WHEN WORDS FAIL

Knowledge Production Through
Practice-Based Art, Design, and Education

SET MARGINS' #79

Ninety-five Theses: When Words Fail

Diplorama! The works featured in the following pages are thesis projects, conceived and developed by ninety-eight young artists and designers from the BA in Design and Art and the MA in Eco-Social Design at the Free University of Bozen-Bolzano, between November 2024 and July 2025. They did not emerge from a predefined theme—such as the "failure of words"—but from research paths independently chosen by each student, each culminating in a thesis as the final synthesis of their studies. At the same time, these works resonate with the central question posed by the volume, offering a common thread across the diverse urgencies they articulate in relation to our present: questioning the speed of technological development, advocating for a more responsible use of resources and consumer goods, critiquing traditional patriarchal structures in family and society, addressing the information overload that defines daily life, or exploring the need to reconnect with one's country of origin after migration.

Through a practice-based approach to knowledge, these projects engage with the present and attempt to formulate temporary solutions for living and navigating it collectively. Taken together, they represent a kind of time capsule of the past year.

The following pages provide only a preview of these works, which can be explored in greater depth through the Faculty's online portfolio: https://designart.unibz.it.

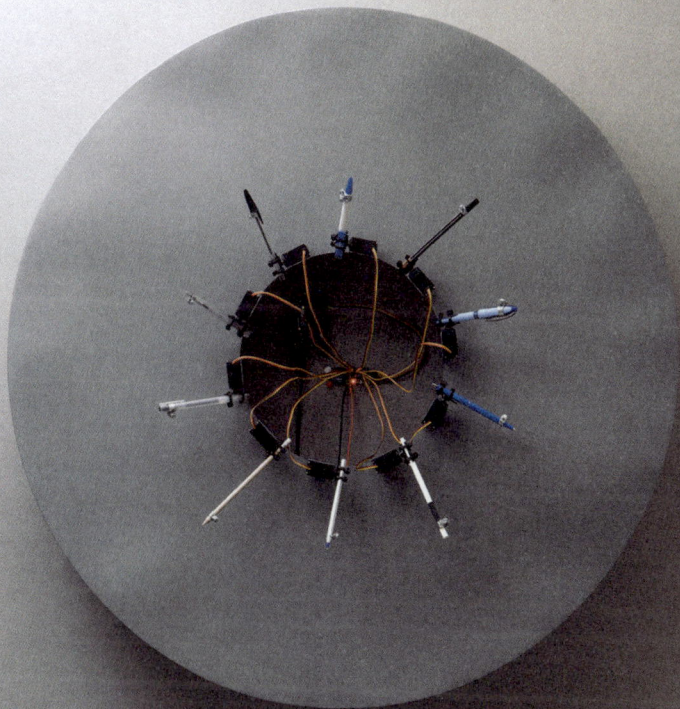

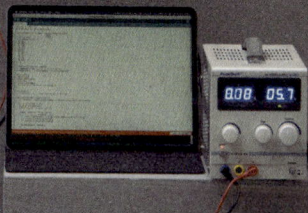

→ p. 140

→ p. 144

→ P. 153

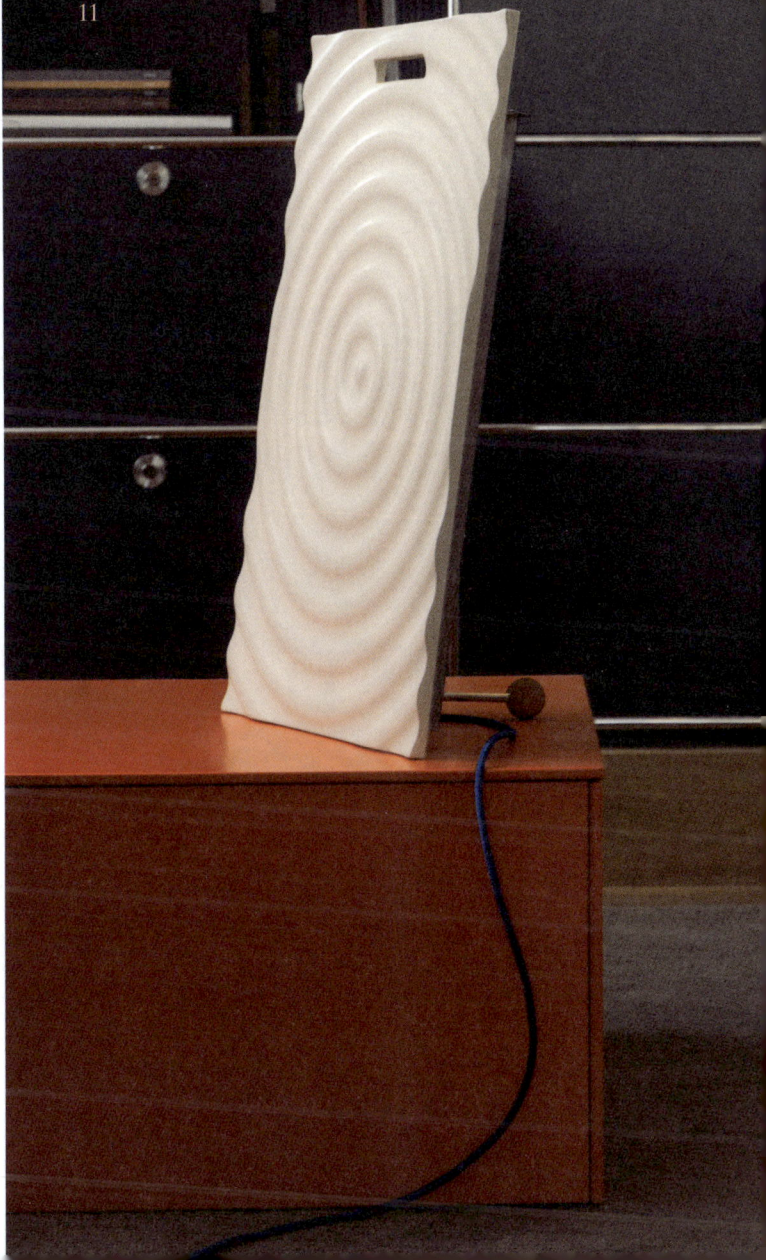

→ P. 123

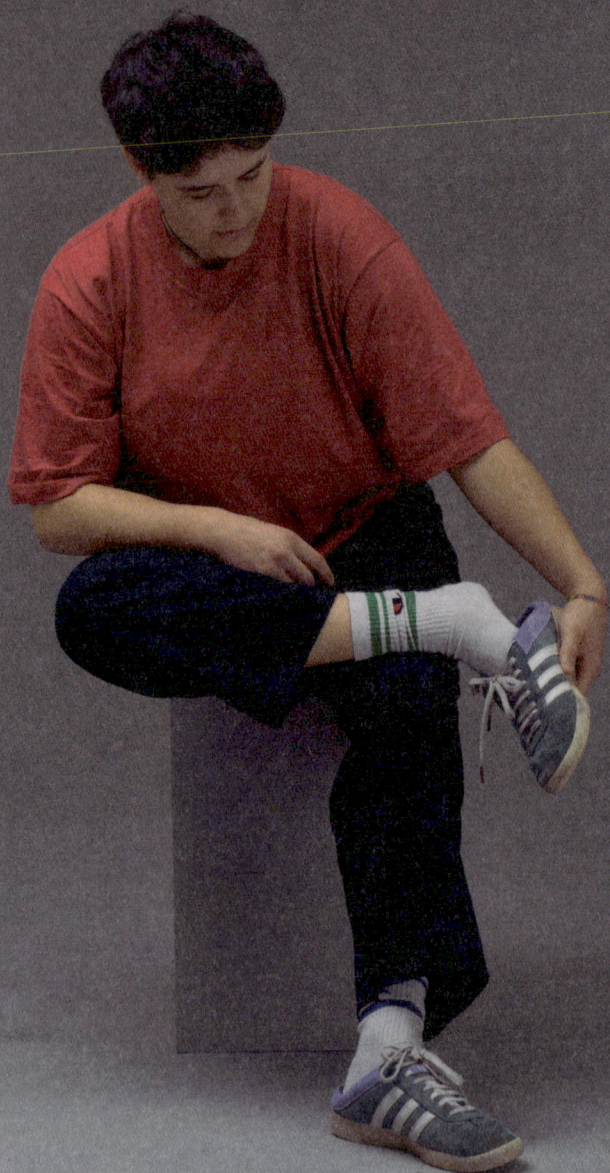

Ismaele Gregori, *Re-Gazelle*

→ p. 132

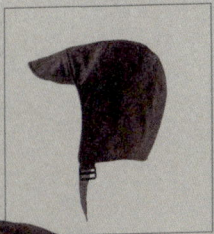

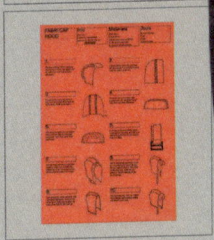

→ p. 115

→p. 116

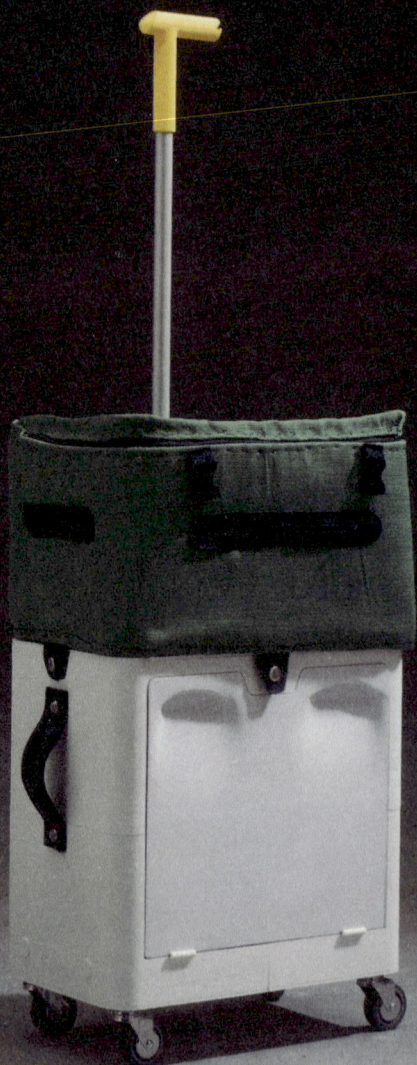

→ p. 124

→p. 131

→ p. 152

Katharina Mercedes Alexandra Schwab, *Greet the Grief*

→ p. 117

Gianluca Norcia, *Unimakers*

→ p. 111

ZEGGALE

→ p. 130

Nicola Parise, *Is It Really Our Duty to Add Fresh Ruins to the Field of Ruins?*

→ p. 145

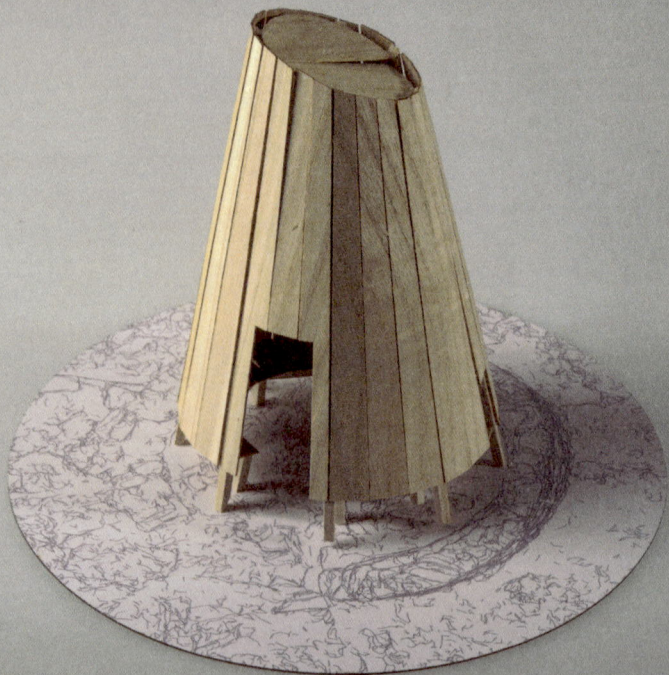

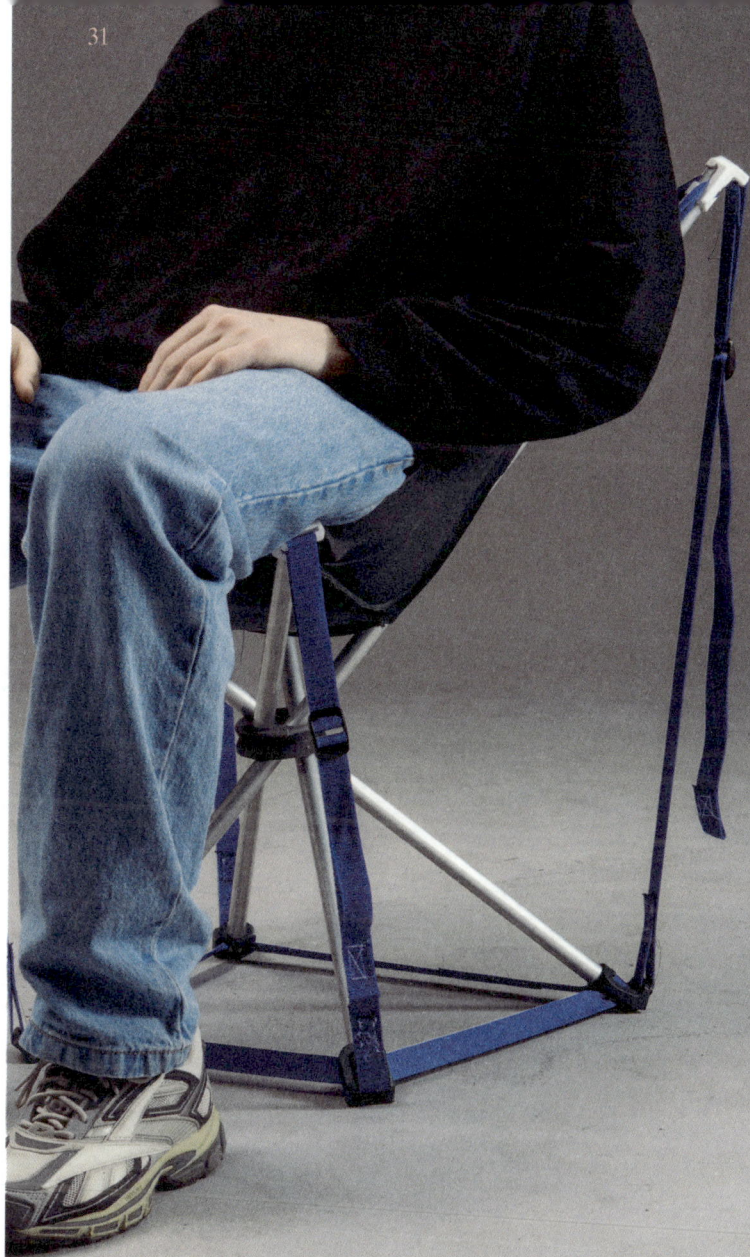

— p. 146

Angela Colapaoli, *centoottantametriquadri*

— p. 122

→ p. 131

→ p. 140

→ p. 154

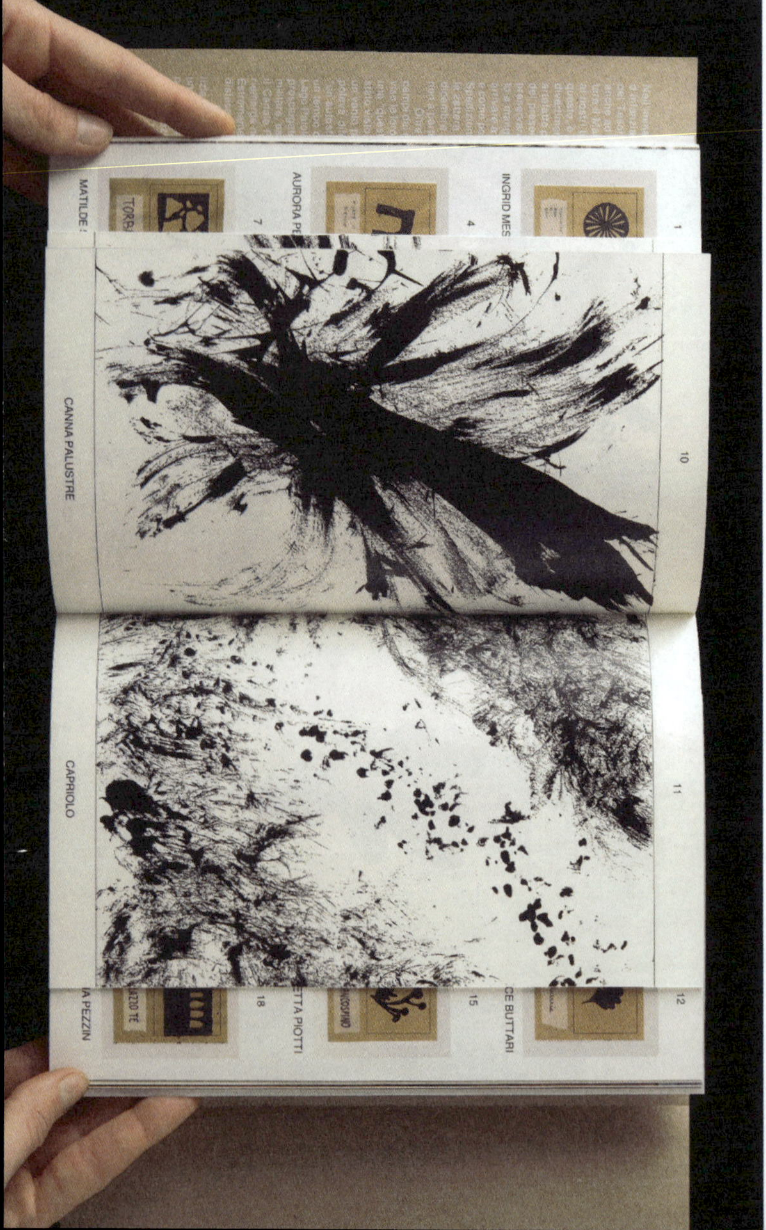
10
CANNA PALUSTRE
11
CAPRIOLO

→ p. 123

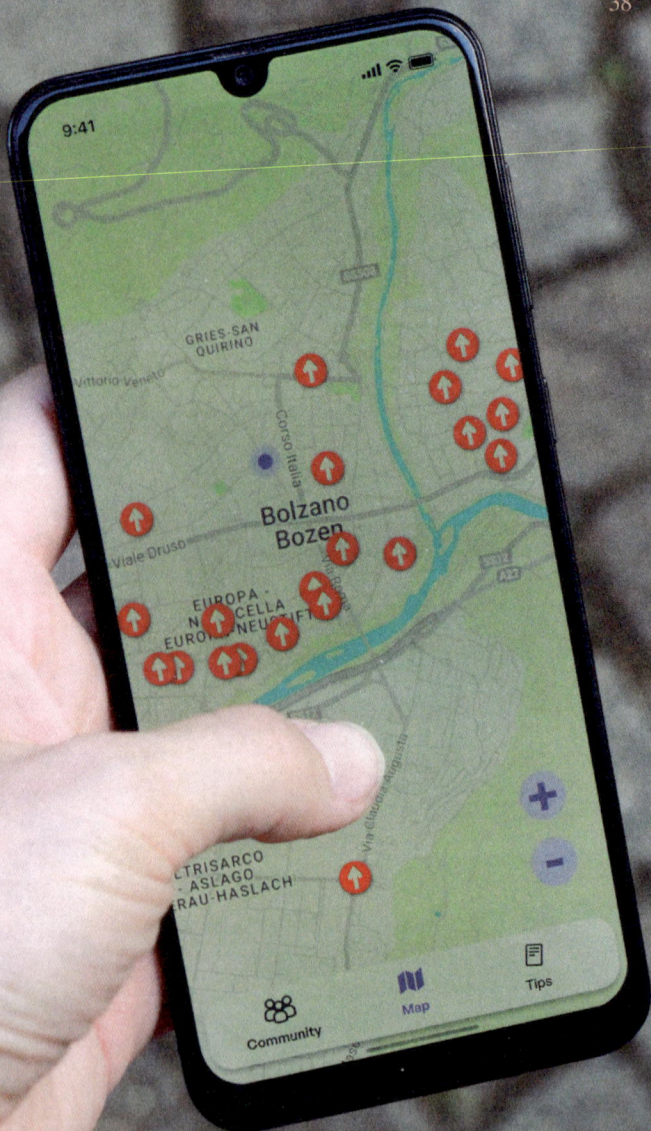

Emma Boaro, *ConCura*

↑ Traghetto di Leonardo, Imbersago (LC)

↑ Scorcio

↑ Fiume Adda, Brivio (LC)

Theresa Felicia Handig, *Hallo, Ich* Menstruiere*

MENSTRUATIONS
PHASE

...eflexion

HALLO, ICH* MENSTRUIERE

Ein Guide über den Menstruationszyklus

FO
P

Soziale Aktivitäten

OVULATIONS
PHASE

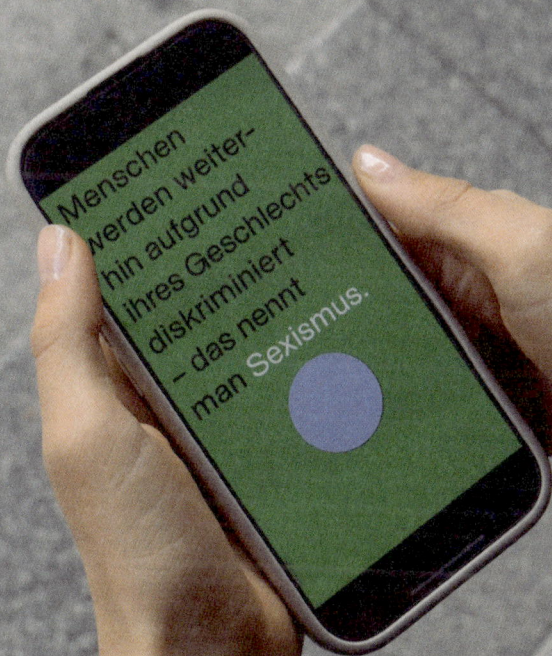

Menschen werden weiterhin aufgrund ihres Geschlechts diskriminiert – das nennt man Sexismus.

→ p. 128

→ P. 156

→ p. 142

VIGO DI FASSA ⸻ CIAMPEDIE, 1965-1988

FIG. 205

FIG. 204

FIG. 203

[FIG. 203] La stazione a valle della funivia di Vigo di Fassa, la partenza avviene direttamente dal centro urbano a 1.382 m. La cabina e in sosta con i passeggeri a bordo. Foto, Vigo di Fassa, settembre 1988.

[FIG. 204] Foto della vista interna della cabina della funivia di Vigo di Fassa durante il viaggio, con a bordo un gruppo di turisti intenti ad osservare il paesaggio dalla grande finestra panoramica. Foto, Vigo di Fassa, settembre 1988.

[FIG. 205] La stazione a monte con cabina della funivia Vigo di Fassa-Ciampedie, nel gruppo del Catinaccio. La funivia inaugurata nel 1965 fu aggiornata nel 1985 con un sistema bifune. Foto, Ciampedie, settembre 1988.

→ p. 152

→ p. 115

Clara Di Liberto, *Fiumāzi*

de_nsolar
des-ciolar

nsolar
nciolar

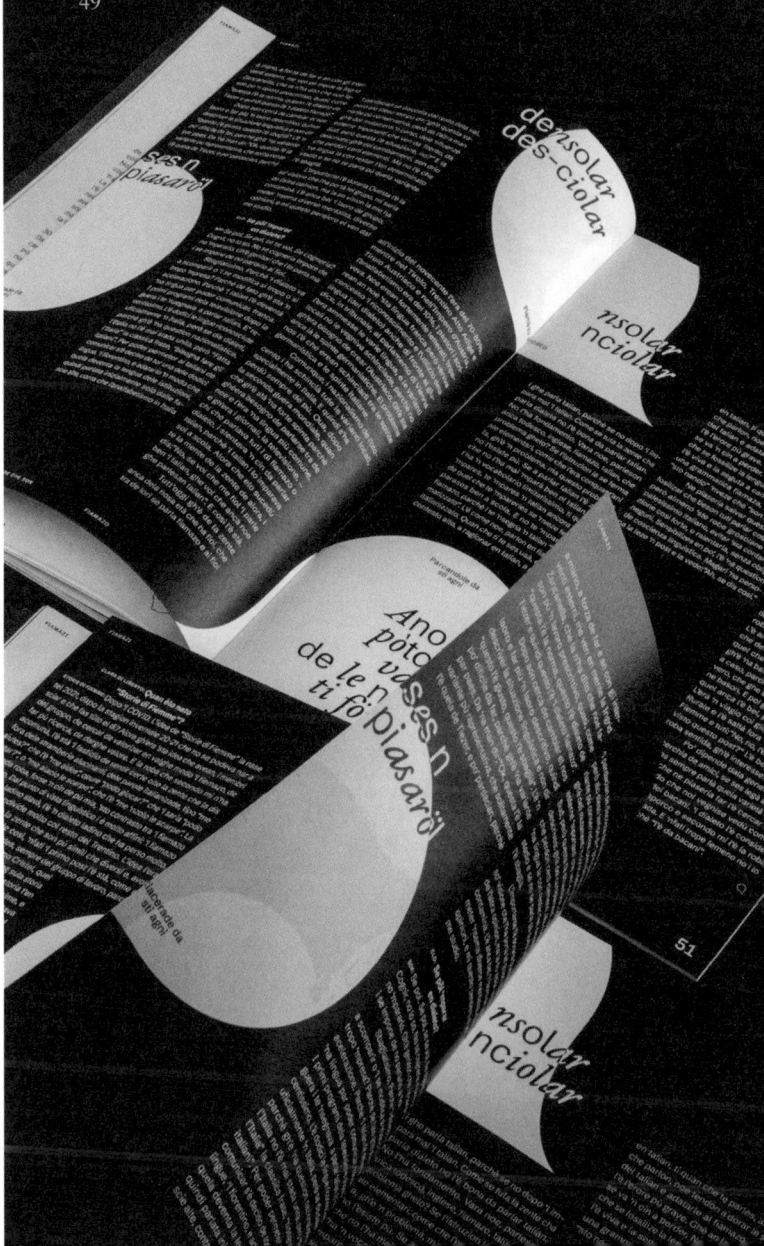

Ano
poto
vases n
de le n
ti fo piasarö

nsolar
nciolar

→ p. 126

— p. 130

...eschichtlicher
...text

...en Spiele und Anla-
... als ein Apell an die
...werden, Deutschland
...Kreis der zivilisierten
...nehmen. «

...er 2001

→ p. 119

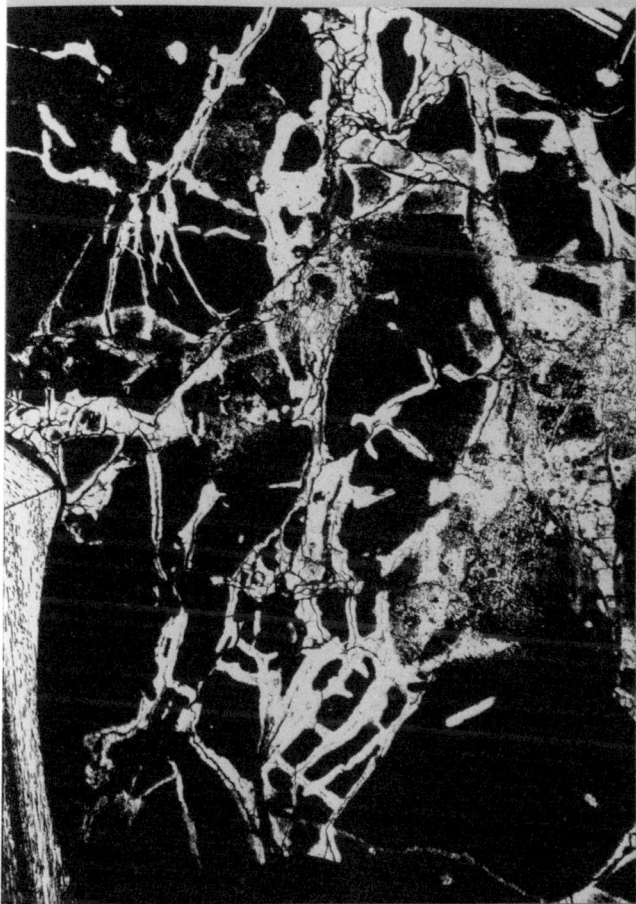

→ P. 155

55

…delines

18.

17:00 – 2…

19.09.

10:00 – 12:00

13:00 – 14…

15:00

19

20.09.

Jury

Chiara Bruned

Isabelle Martinod

Franziska Weber

Anita De Rosat

Ilya Petrooz

Giulia Ferrara

Focus Urbano

Centre Européen de la Photographie

Martin Parr Foundation

Fondazione Morra Luce

Bellucce Contemporary Photography Forum

Candidate Magazine

SUBMIT NOW

About   Edition 2027   Program   Artists   Winners   FAQ

Editions

2026 Appearance

Who are we ?
Meet the team.

Francesca Chiachio

Francesco Gioia

Antoine Souhayl

Ne…

Chris Yan

ght

e artificiale

...zionato il nostro modo
...vivere, ma risulta spesso eccessiva
e mal progettata ...dosi
verso il cielo, e ...desiderate
anziché concen... rve.

**Inquiname...
lumin...**

È il termine utilizzato per descriv...
...esto fenomeno nelle sue diverse
...ifestazioni, spe... comuni
...e passare i... ai più.

Cosa perdiamo quando
illuminiamo il buio?

→ p. 124

E provò

Msna

Guide

→ p. 141

→ p. 129

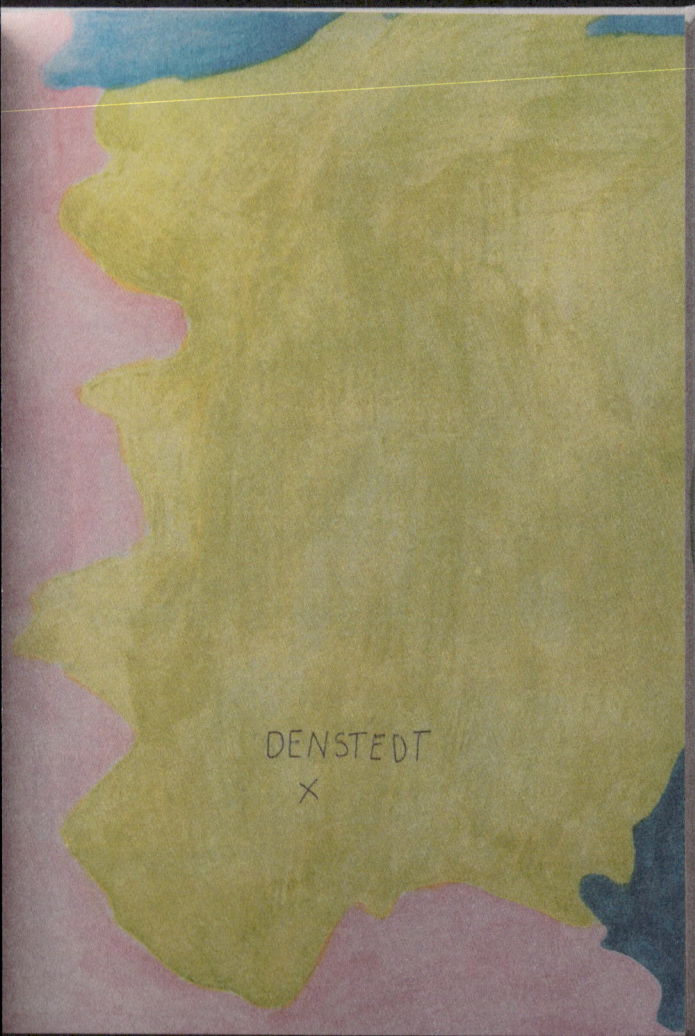

DENSTEDT
X

Rosa Maja Klingholz, *Im Garten der DDR*

—p. 136

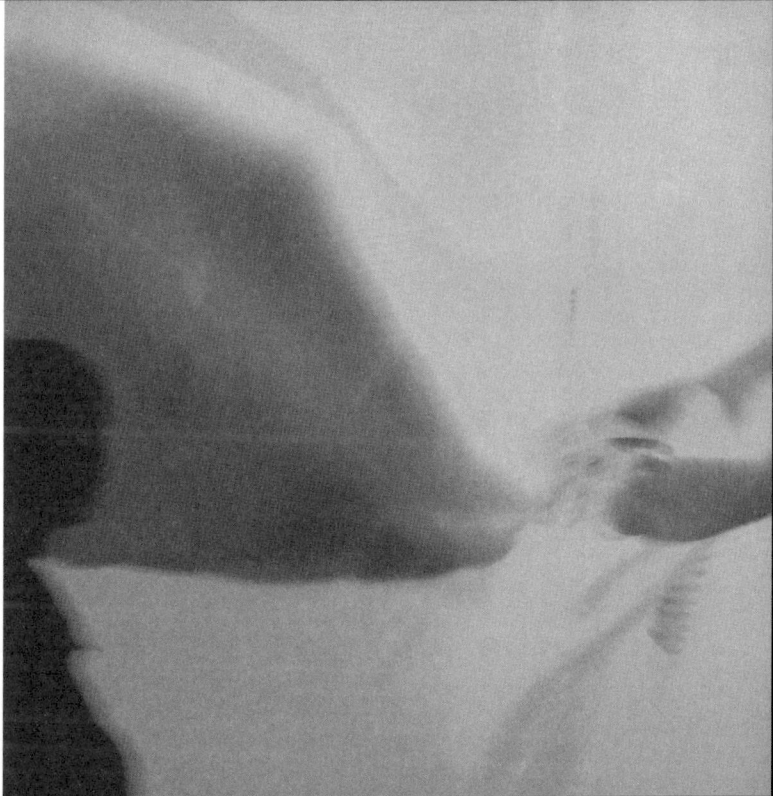

Grete Henriette Rederer, *Aftertouch Vol. 1*

— p. 149

→ p. 141

→p. 120

Ariana Georgiana Mirea, *Totu Moare în România*

→p. 142

Katharina Maria Hanglberger, *I'd Rather Be a Father*

→p. 133

→ p. 111

→ p. 110

-June 10
LIVE L.A.
700 Marines
Deployed to
L.A. After
Night of
Protests

Our 21 Best
Chocolate
Chip Cookie
Recipes

Dopo gli attacchi di Israele

l'Iran issa la

'bandiera rossa

della vendetta'

14.06.25

22.06.25
US officially enters war,

Iran vows:'You will pay'

—p. 117

→p. 119

Francesca Cantele, *Spettri*

→ p. 113

REFLECTI-
ON

→ p. 135

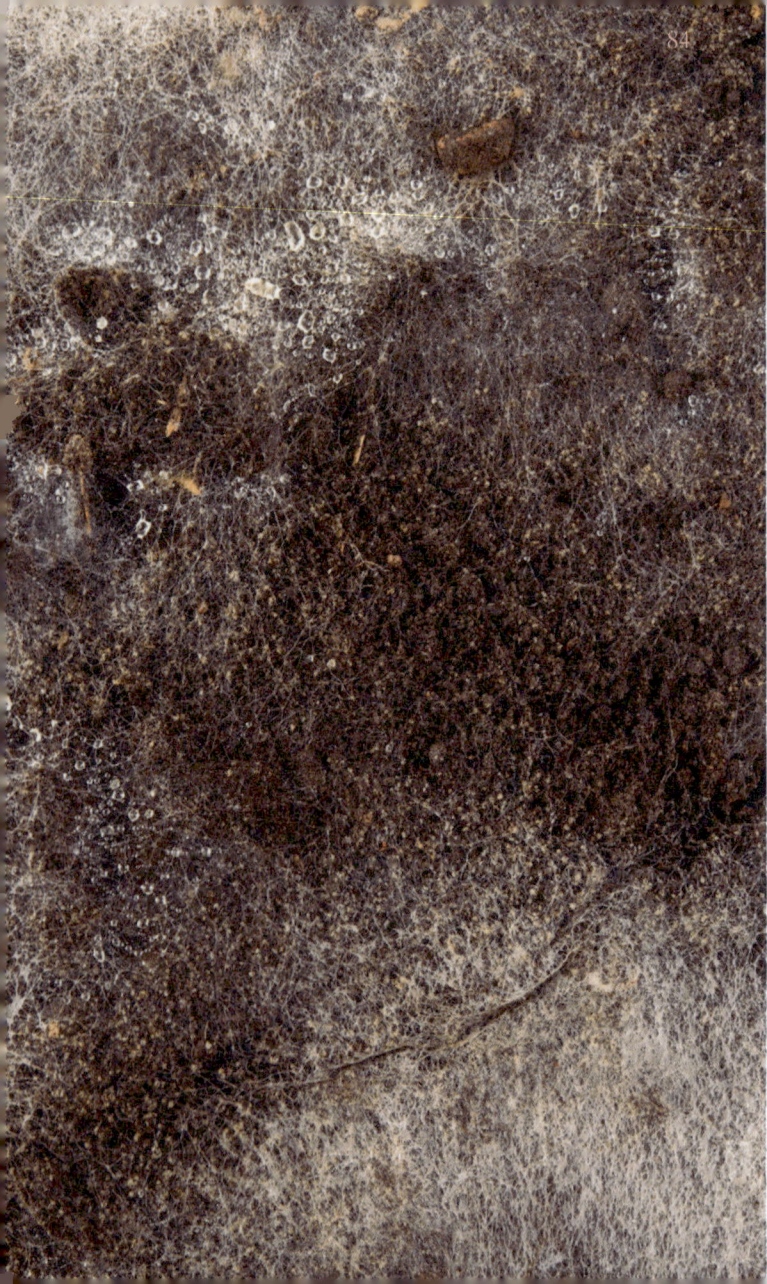

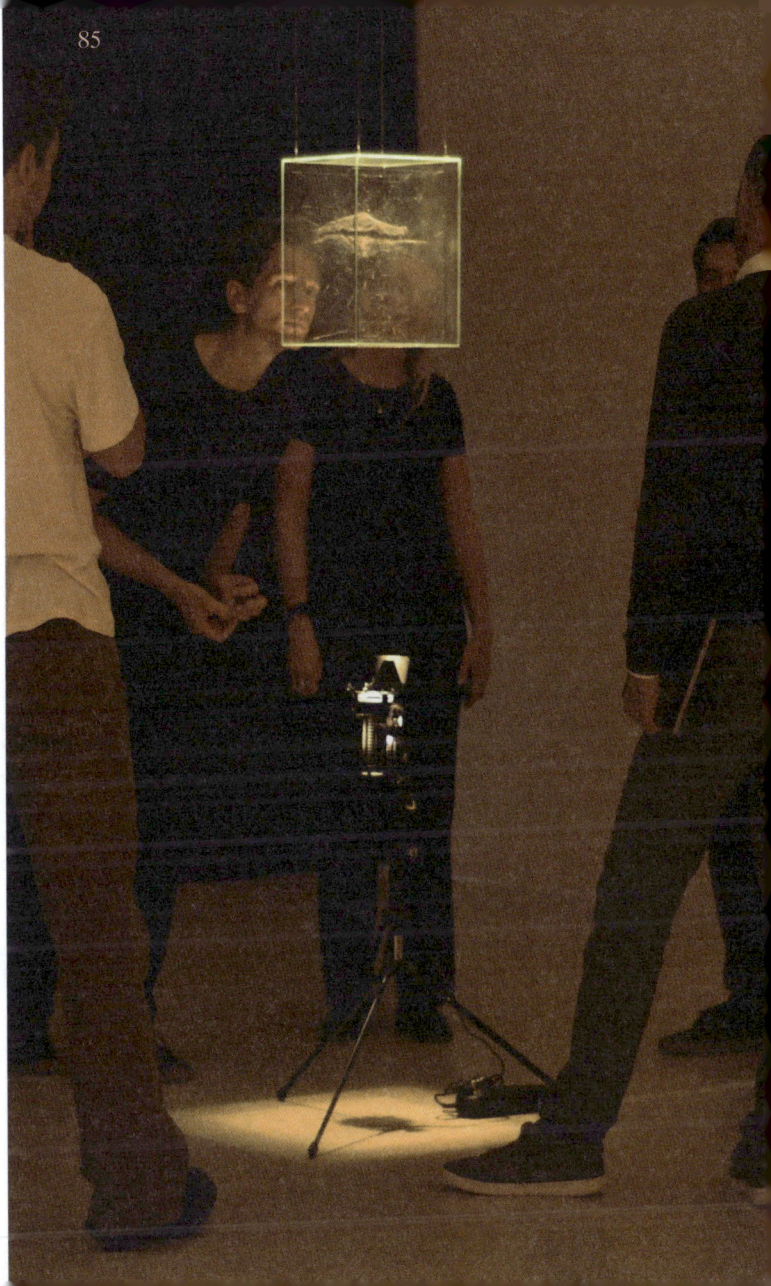

→ p. 135

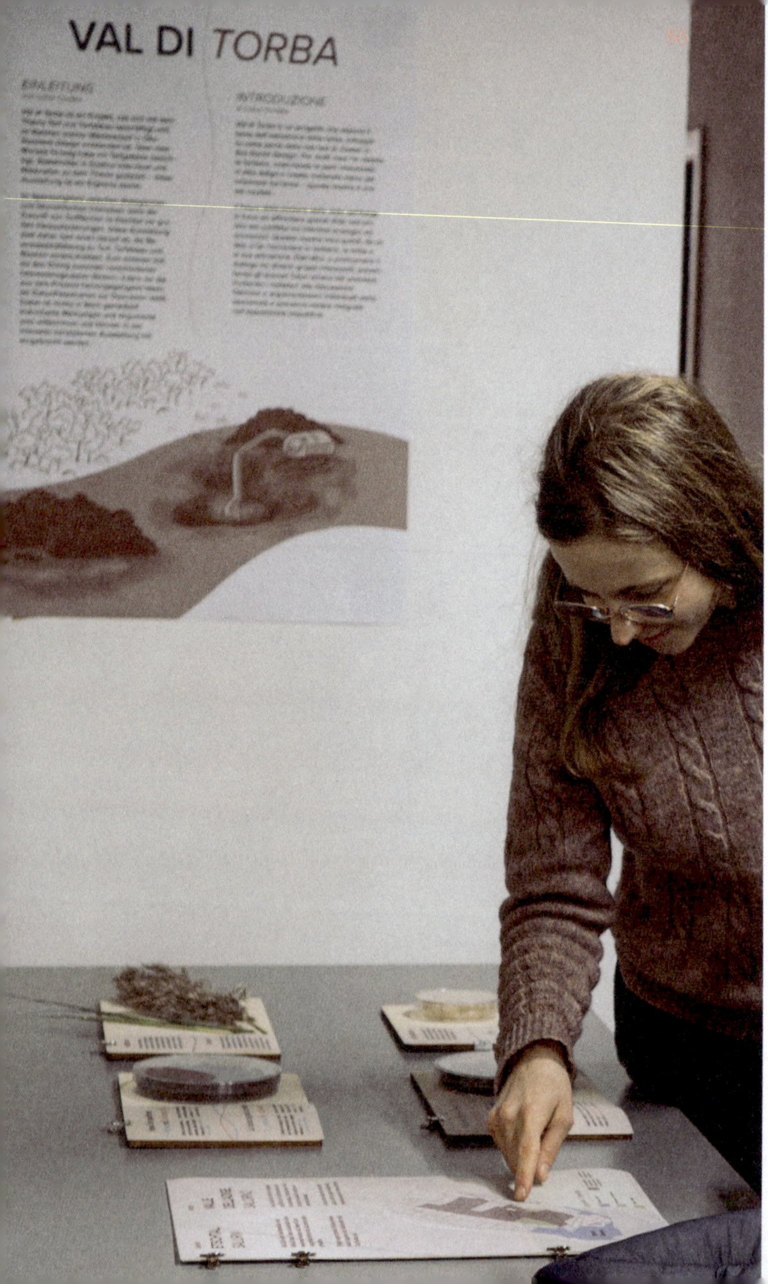

Laïsa Sophie Cordes, *Val di Torba*

→ p. 122

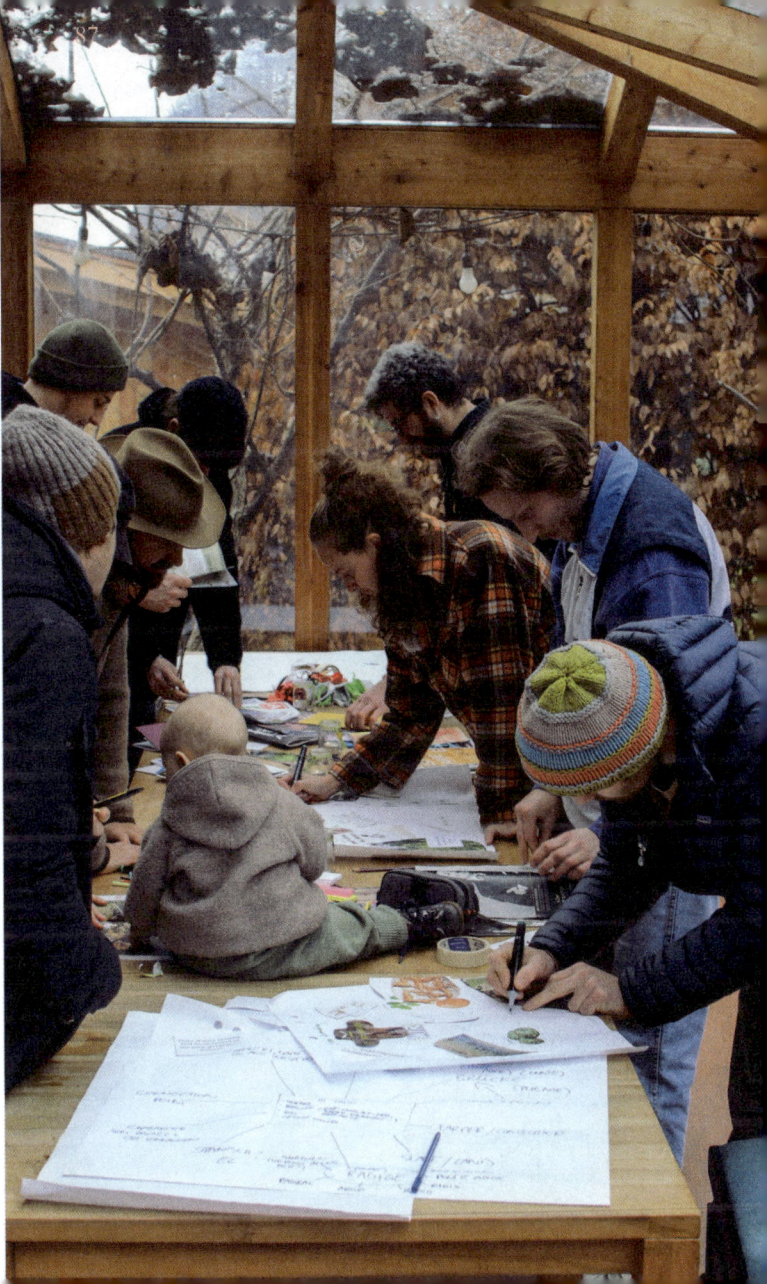

Koenraad Gerardus Reerink, *Plot Twist*

Sei dabei und gestalte mit
– im Gespräch, mit Ideen, mit Herz!

Ein Pilotprojekt zur ländlichen
Entwicklung im Allgäu

→ P. 128

— p.112

A Bolzano, cosa ti sembra
difficile da raggiungere?

Quali sono le
piacciono a

un immigrato,
uno straniero?

Crea un collage di emoji
della vita scolastica di tutti
i giorni.

Disegna una cartolina che
mostri ciò che ti piace di
Bolzano.

Quali sono
tua vi
genit

Quando indossi l'abito
tradizior
cultura f

ove ti vedi dopo la scuola?

ale lingua sogni?

Dove hai la sensazione di
poter essere te stessa/o?

In Quali situazioni ti sei
sentita/o trattata/o
ingiustamente nel passato
Secondo te, qual era il
motivo o la causa di questo

Disegna una etichetta
tradizionale della bevanda
della tua famiglia.

Redini con una bevanda
della tua famiglia.

Disegna un'etichetta di
Nutella con le cose che ti
rendono unico/a.

Crea un collage di emoji su
come pensi che sia il nostro
futuro.

Quali sono le cose che
piacciono a Bolzano

della
cosono le trad'
tua famigli
piaccio

elle chiari
osi, Belli
pensi?

Com'è diverso il
di amici a scuola r
quello fuori

Crea una storia emoji con le
sensazioni che provi
riguardo a ciò che non li
piace di Bolzano.

glia.

chetta
la cultura
bevanda

Mostraci la tua cronologia di
ricerca su Google.

Qual è stata la
bugna

Disegna un'etichetta con tre desideri
Nutella con i tuoi futuro.

gina
con le
accadrà dopo
Conserval
indica
Crea una capsula di
accadrà dopo il tempo
che

I GIOVANI COME RIPRESA E RISORSA

unibz
Freie Universität Bozen
Libera Università di Bolzano
Università Liedia de Bulsan

gener
azioni

Bureaucracy makes beasts of us all. scared, or hunted, or the

The Sluggish

16 months. 1 years 3 hours under the sun.

They move, eventually. But on their time — not on yours. And in their delay, you want, you pause.

YOUR TIME

...RK CORRECT BRIDGE

(...RARILY STABLE — PROCEED WITH CAUTION)

→ p. 125

—p. 134

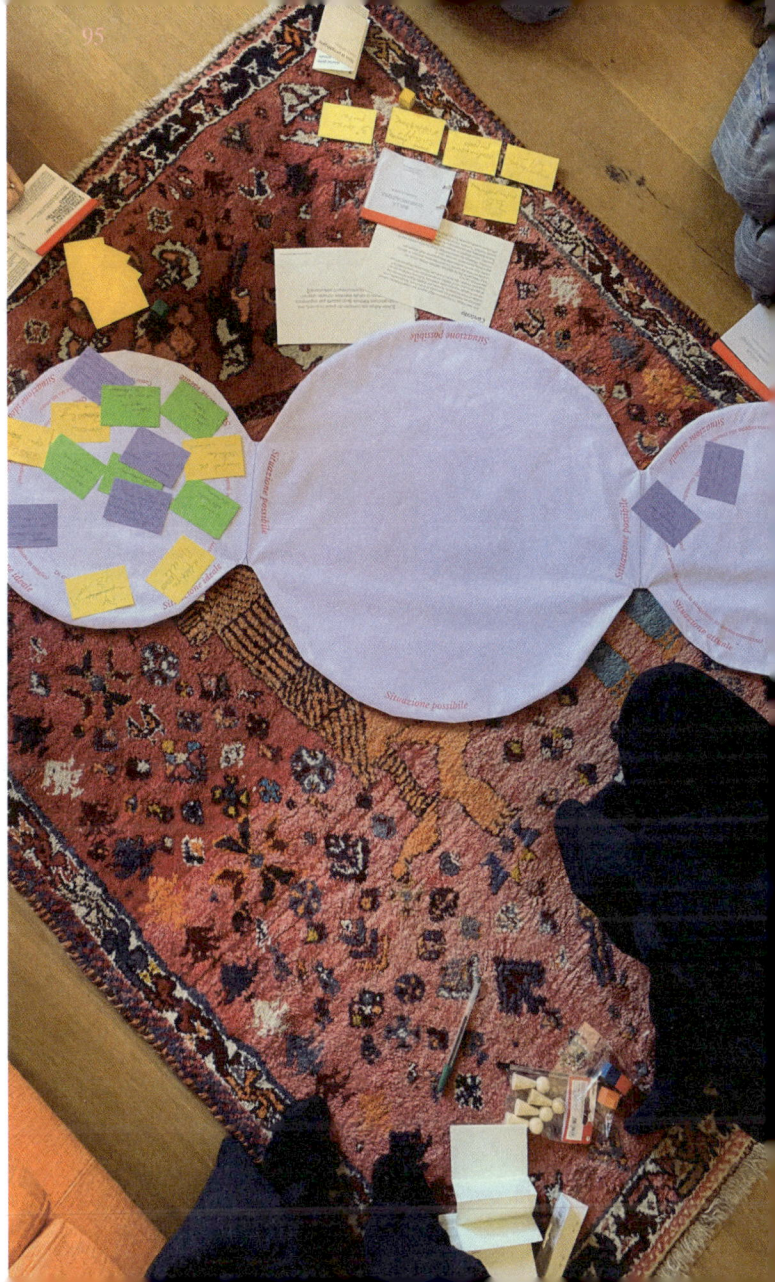

wor(l)d guiding
An introduction

Open-source plug-ins for
institutions. An
by maja hauke

lear... circl...
Allowing a sh...

Open so...
institut...
institutions. A...
ja hauke an...

not only, but also
...about more-than-western episte...

...en-source plug-ins for educat...
...stitutions. An exchange and co...
maja hauke and miela salgado

from object to matter
A plug-in for conserving, imagining beyond
and relating with

Open-sou...
institutio...
by maja h...

with whom & from where?
Revealing the particular & positi...

...ource plug-ins for educ...
...ions. An exchange and
...xchange and miela sa...

→ p. 134

d Raum zum Austausch.

In den frühen Tagen von Sounds True
brachte Tami Simon, die Gründerin u...
CEO, ihren Hund mit ins Büro. Einige
...eiter fragten bald, ob sie auch ihr...
...en dürften. Tami sah ...abzulehnen,
...er locker
...fen und du bist

...ass in
...dabei

Wir (Team/Mitarbeiter)
haben genug Zeit und
Raum zum Austausch.

...beitern.
...in der
...er ist.
...um
...eines
...sst
...ben.

...ollegen
...ganz subtil
...eidung, die
...hen, brachte nicht
...sondern auch mehr
...Leben.

→ p. 157

CRITICAL
UKRAINIAN
GARDENS

eco-social workbook
winter 2025 edition
edited by yeva kupchenko

→p. 146

My HS* Experience

Field research

In November, I lived with two host families for a total of 15 days. I worked for them for an average 4 hours a day, 5 days a week, in exchange for room and board to have a better understanding of the HS dinamics.

Goldfish Family

06-13 Nov. 24   Language: IT   ● = family color

Members

Accomodation
Private room and bathroom.

HS History
5 yrs. experience as a Host.
20+ people hosted

Reason
Getting to know new cultures. Need for help with children

Hotwheels Family

18-26 Nov. 24   Language: IT, ENG   ● = family color

Members

Accomodation
Semi-private depandance with indipendent entrance.

HS History
6 yrs. experience as a Host.

Reason
After traveling a lot in life, feeling like giving back to others.

Work-leisu...

House's Emotional Map

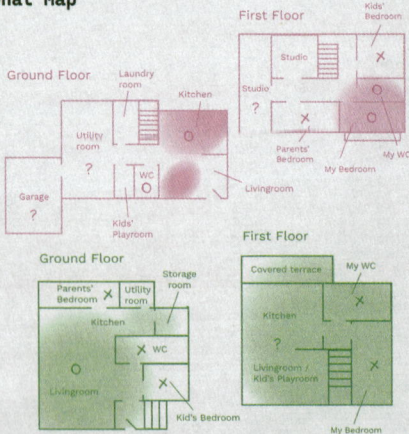

Chart Legend

● = GF Family
● = HW Family

Comfort:

? = Unclear rules for accessing these rooms
✗ = Unspoken rules for accessing these rooms
○ = Clearified rules for accessing these rooms

Ground Floor — Laundry room, Kitchen, Utility room, WC, Garage, Kids' Playroom

First Floor — Kids' Bedroom, Studio, Studio, Parents' Bedroom, My WC, My Bedroom, Livingroom

Ground Floor — Parents' Bedroom, Utility room, Storage room, Kitchen, WC, Livingroom, Kid's Bedroom

First Floor — Covered terrace, My WC, Kitchen, Livingroom / Kid's Playroom, My Bedroom

Tasks and D...

Cooking

Running Errands

House Maintainances

→ p. 126

70

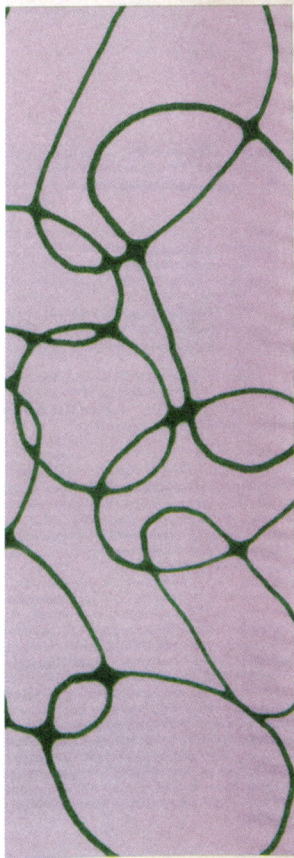

1. Constella

CREATING RELATIONAL N

The creation of relational networks within rural
eco-social transformations, therefore beneficial f
interconnected communities. Engaging in the de
conceptualised as the action of creating new poin
stakeholders, represents the primary challenge o
participatory processes in rural territories. Abse
awareness and ability to participate in LANDSCAPE
resulting in the bias and non-reflective nature of

At a national level, territorial development polici
abandonment of Italian inner areas providing fie
is required, with a design rewarding public and p
of such areas of intervention include cultural pas
of local heritage, digitalisation, and the increase
consolidated top-down territorial planning mode
actions to simplistic and univocal ones without a
local dimension (Bindi et al., 2022), yet engender
and public feeling, and accordingly from public

In contrast, the creation of bottom-up relational
factor in initiating public participation processes
residents. This approach both encourages the rea
platform for dialogue and imaginative work, whi
process through power redistribution (Arnstein,
the needs of inhabitants are the requirements fo
areas. The process of bringing together different
of inhabitants, systematizing them, and initiating
for the co-creation of potential future rural lands
to encourage more dialogue-oriented local netwo
of community and belonging among residents, as
in landscape governance.

In scenarios where such participatory practices a
in dialogue with local inhabitants, the integratio
knowledge is fundamental (Bodorkós and Pataki,
to happen, several critical contingent factors refe
the careful use of language that respects and alig
of the context, and a deliberate and pace that res
of the community.

→ p. 145

→ p. 139

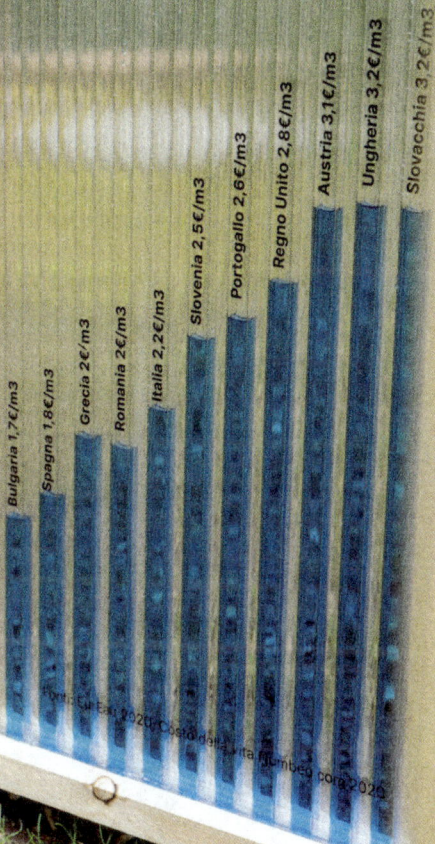

Bulgaria 1,7€/m3
Spagna 1,8€/m3
Grecia 2€/m3
Romania 2€/m3
Italia 2,2€/m3
Slovenia 2,5€/m3
Portogallo 2,6€/m3
Regno Unito 2,8€/m3
Austria 3,1€/m3
Ungheria 3,2€/m3
Slovacchia 3,2€/m3

Eugenia Pinna

On Monday 23 December 2025 I trave
to Nule. Nule is famous for being the

Fig. 41

Ethnographic research

dolaptan çıkanlar

dolaba hoşgeldin! burası sana
bana bize ait bir alan. dolapta
gördüklerin, kuir öznesi bireylerin
özellikle trans+ deneyimlerin giyim
ve görsel ifade pratikleri üzerinden

anlatımları ve biriktirmeleridir.
deneyim ve hikaye paylaşımlarını
teşvik ettiğimiz bu alanı şimdilik
üç ayrı şeyin içinde biriktiriyoruz:
bir dikiş kutusu, bir valiz, ve
bir hediye paketi. bu eşyaların
içlerine bakıp neler sakladıklarını

keşfedebilir, ve kendi eşya ve anılarınla
dolaba kendinden bir şey ekleyebilirsin.

bu çalışma kapsamında toplanan
hikayeler tamamen anonimdir, çalışma
herhangi bir kişisel veri (isim, e-mail, vb.)
toplamaz. yapılan paylaşımlar değerlen-
dirildikten sonra varılan koleksiyona
dahil edilir ve kolektif dolabın
bir parçası olur. bu süreçte kıyafet,

as long as it is not deleted. Inside the smartphone, the feeling of loss may not exist. Everything is salvageable, everything is retrievable if conditions allow. The continuous availability of the means enables us to be continuously collecting personal information. One can always produce and consume without significant limits.

This is a one portrayal of the smartphone.

What is presence today?
What is my smartphone to me?

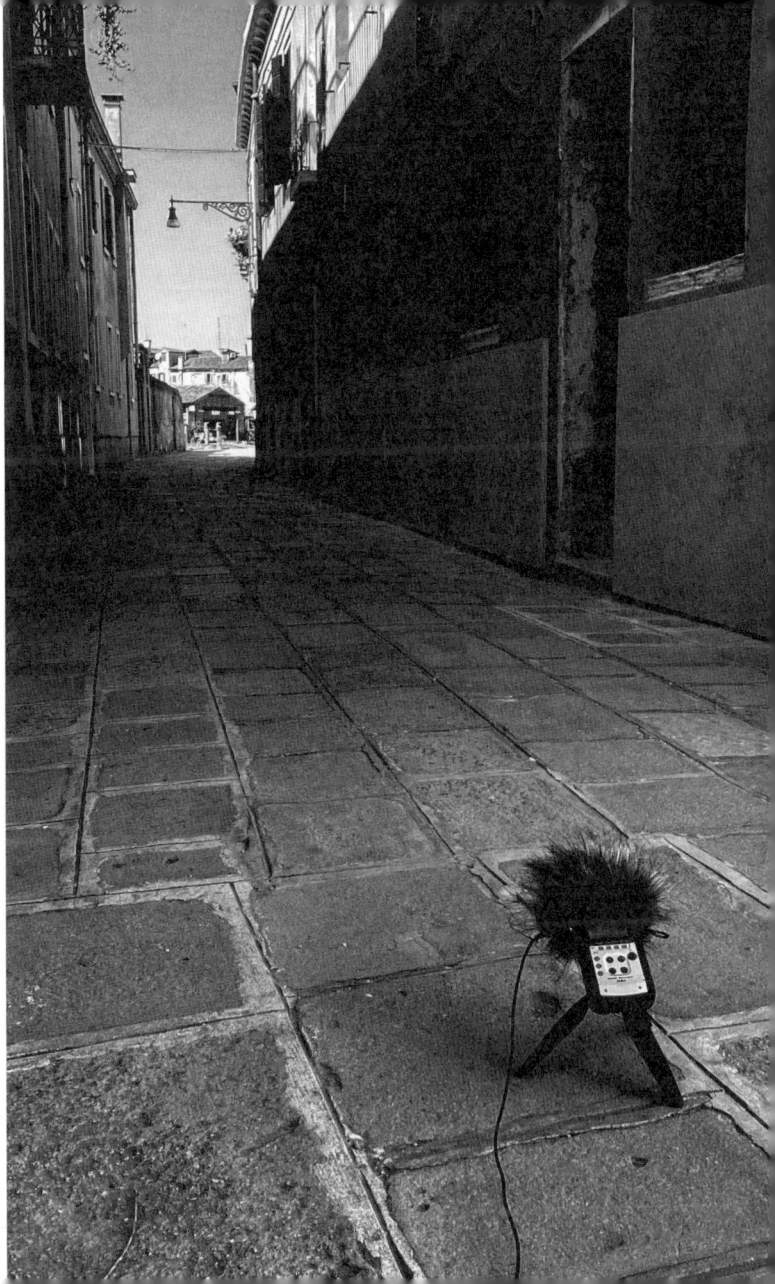

→p.121

Solveigh Isabel Artschwager
Dance Beyond Form: Water Leather Bags Are Walking in Space
Supervisors: Davide Tommaso Ferrando, Dana Iova-Koga

Inci Aslan
Remediation Network: Developing a Systemic Pathways to Environmental Recovery by Using Fungal Bioremediation Practices
Supervisors: Camilo Ayala Garcia, Lorenza Conterna

Dance Beyond Form explores Butoh —an avant-garde Japanese performance form that emerged in the 1960s and spread globally—as a universal language capable of fostering intercultural dialogue. The research investigates whether the primal movements of Butoh can reflect shared human emotions and experiences, strengthening social bonds and mutual understanding across cultures. Inspired by Butoh's poetic vision of the human being as a water-filled leather bag moved by gravity, the project engaged three different communities through collaborative and performative practices, addressing themes of nomadic life, European cultural exchange, and death rituals. Each encounter culminated in a "Butoh Walk": a bodily metamorphosis shaped by the interplay of material forces (climate and landscape), social forces (languages, rhythms, and hierarchies), and imaginal forces (myths and collective memories). From this process, key questions arise: Can Butoh become a global grammar of feelings? And how do cultural and environmental contexts shape this embodied language?

The Remediation Network project addresses polluted landscapes where ecological damage is closely entangled with political, economic, and historical forces of neglect. Taking mycelium—often celebrated as a "material of the future"—as its starting point, the project explores whether this living network can become an ally in the slow and uneven processes of remediation. By cultivating mycelium on agricultural byproducts, the project investigates how waste can be transformed into a resource for ecological regeneration. Moving between laboratory experiments and field practices, and combining material exploration with dialogue among farmers, scientists, and local communities, it envisions a distributed remediation network based on open-source protocols and locally available materials. Rather than an exercise in technological optimism, the project develops a critical inquiry into who defines contamination, who takes responsibility for repair, and what forms of knowledge shape environmental recovery.

→ p. 74

→ p. 84

Sofia Aspromonte
Gioca con me – Una collezione: The Design of Board Games Applied in Social Care for Patients with Alzheimer's, Dementia, and Senile Dementia

Supervisors: Eduardo Martins Guerra, Marcello Barison

The world is undergoing a profound demographic shift: over the next forty years, the global elderly population is projected to rise from six hundred million to over two billion, surpassing the number of young people. This transformation is reshaping social models and redefining elderly care. Modern retirement homes are no longer solely focused on physical health but also on dignity, interpersonal connection, and psychological well-being. Drawing on personal experience, my project *Gioca con me* ("Play with Me") explores the role of board-games in dementia care. Through an in-depth analysis of patients' needs, it seeks to reorganize spaces, materials, and activities to address gaps caused by misinformation and limited resources. The collection adapts traditional games into tools for emotional regulation, cognitive stimulation, and crisis prevention. By integrating play into therapeutic programs, the project enhances daily routines, promoting recreation, social interaction, and quality of life for people with dementia.

→ p. 26

Carmine Auricchio
Buon sangue non mente

Supervisors: Eva Leitolf, Elisabetta Rattalino

Buon sangue non mente ("Good Blood Doesn't Lie") is a photographic project that investigates identity dynamics and psychological legacies within the extended family. The title directly references a popular saying that links destiny and character to lineage, while simultaneously questioning its validity. The project overturns traditional family expectations typical of sociocultural contexts such as Southern Italian urban outskirts, where the role of the "male heir" has historically entailed significant identity pressures. The photographs thus take shape as a "family mythology," where individual perception redefines and at times distorts the reality of the subjects. Through a series of carefully constructed portraits, the work explores mechanisms of projection and subjective perception, articulated through formal choices that render each image a symbolic and interpretative vision of the subjects portrayed. The work highlights how identity and personality are deeply shaped by family projections and upbringing, producing internal structures that can mark and deform the self.

→ pp. 70–71

Giorgia Baccichetti
Punto d'Incontro: Transforming Disability Perception through Learning and Playing

Supervisors: Sónia Cabral Matos, Heidrun Demo

The project *Punto d'Incontro* ("Meeting point") explores people's perceptions of disability and how to counteract exclusionary attitudes by fostering a culture of inclusion from an early age. Aimed at children aged nine to eleven—before social biases are fully internalized—the project seeks to reduce the distance between children and disability, promoting empathy, active listening, and multi-channel communication. The outcome is an educational game designed as a practical tool for teachers and educators to introduce these themes in a simple, engaging manner. The project serves as a starting point: a small spark with which to light meaningful dialogue on disability and diversity in the classroom.

→ p. 89

Sophia Basso
The Shape of Imagination: How perception transforms visual noise into meaning

Supervisors: Andreas Trenker, Marcello Barison

The project investigates the role of imagination and visual perception in contemporary society through the phenomenon of pareidolia—the tendency to recognize familiar forms in random patterns, such as faces in car fronts or cloud formations. In a context where modern life often prioritizes productivity, success, and education, imagination risks being undervalued. This work asks how perception can be sharpened, how the familiar might be reframed, and where sources of inspiration for imagination can be found. The work takes the form of a catalogue of pareidolia, made up of photographs and images to be expanded through interpretative readings, revealing hidden characters and stories within the undefined. By translating perception into visual form, the project proposes new modes of communication and ways of seeing. Pareidolia becomes a tool for evoking memories, sparking narratives, and reclaiming imagination as an essential resource in today's fast-paced world.

→ p. 53

Lucas Batliner
Von der Bilderwelt der Weltbilder des Matthias Schönweger
Supervisors: Shona Kitchen, Markus Schlaffke

This thirty-five-minute documentary/artist's film offers an intimate look into the ideas behind the paintings, performances, books, and installations of South Tyrolean artist Matthias Schönweger. It provides insight into his worldview—ranging from geopolitical concerns to local cultural and international themes—while inviting viewers to explore fragments of his reality. Like Schönweger's own practice, the film *Von der Bilderwelt der Weltbilder des Matthias Schönweger* ("From the Pictorial World of Matthias Schönweger's Worldviews") can be approached superficially but also reveals deeper layers upon closer observation. It weaves together scenes, contrasts, and connections that hold meaning both individually and collectively. Most sequences are carefully constructed, yet always contain an unpredictable element, an unforeseen moment of surprise.

Chiara Christina Baumgärtel
Wortschatz: Kamishibai-Language Stories for Children
Supervisors: Giorgio Camuffo, Gerhard Glüher

Where do letters come from? Why do we call a table "table"? And who had the strange idea of giving the word "scale" two completely different meanings? Language surrounds us everywhere: it shapes our thoughts and feelings, influences our actions, and defines how we perceive the world and connect with others. The project *Wortschatz* ("Vocabulary") is more than an illustrated book. It is both a performative narration technique and a story split into episodes, told through *Kamishibai*: a traditional Japanese form of street theatre. In this adapted version, the story unfolds through illustrated boards displayed in a portable wooden frame. These visual narratives help children develop an early curiosity for language and literature, while playfully transmitting linguistic concepts and enthusiasm that can inspire them to create and tell stories of their own.

→ p. 78   → p. 27

Pier Elia Benetti
Lost in the Light
Supervisors: Giulia Cordin, Christian Upmeier

For centuries, the night sky has been a source of wonder, guiding civilizations, inspiring myths, and fueling discovery. Yet, in our contemporary world, we are slowly losing its significance without even realizing it. Light pollution—the excessive and misdirected artificial light brightening our night skies—is a growing yet under-discussed issue. Its effects disrupt wildlife, interfere with human health and circadian rhythms, waste energy and resources, and lead to a profound cultural loss due to our slowly disappearing ability to connect with the universe. *Lost in the Light* seeks to raise awareness of the pervasive spread of light pollution within the local context of Trentino-Alto Adige, where nature comes up against constant urban expansion, and to explore how this growing issue reduces our connection to the night sky and damages the natural environment. Through visual design, the project will encourage viewers to rediscover an appreciation for the darkness, inviting reflection on the importance of preserving the night sky.

→ p. 56

Sarah Binkowski
Home? Belonging Short Stories
Supervisors: Elisabeth Tauber, Paulina Eberhardt

This project explores belonging through the personal narratives of migrant youth in Bolzano, Italy. Grounded in ethnographic research, it amplifies voices of young people facing marginalization at the intersection of ethnicity, gender, religion, and socioeconomic status. Over six months at the Casetta youth club in Oltrisarco, their stories and interactions were documented. The work critically addresses systemic injustices while fostering agency and a sense of belonging. findings reveal exclusion shaped by race, gender, class, academic performance, and religion. These dynamics restrict opportunities, fuel identity conflicts, and reinforce stereotypes. The education system emerges as a key site of discrimination, while youth also face a lack of safe spaces, economic pressures, and the pursuit of recognition. The project calls for urgent educational reform that embraces diversity and empowers migrant youth to shape their futures. By centering their perspectives, it raises awareness and opens paths to institutional change, reframing belonging as both personal and collective.

→ p. 90

Sofia Biscosi
Da soli siamo invisibili: Ambient Campaign Against Precarious Work
Supervisors: Gianluca Seta, Marcello Barison

Da soli siamo invisibili ("Alone We Are Invisible") is a campaign created to inspire political engagement among workers by exposing the realities of invisible labor—precarious, unregistered, and poverty-wage jobs—using urban spaces as a unique communication medium. Precarious work affects over three million Italians, yet it is often dismissed as an individual problem, trapping workers in a cycle of economic and emotional instability. This isolation prevents many from acknowledging the political nature of the issue and mobilizing for change. The campaign leverages personal stories to underscore a shared struggle, bringing these narratives into public spaces to engage an audience ever harder to reach through traditional media. The campaign's focal point is an urban installation situated in a high-traffic area. Featuring work garments positioned to create the illusion of invisible figures, each outfit symbolizes a worker and is paired with a personal story that unveils class-based contradictions.

→ p. 48

Sören Bläcker
Legno Veloce: Light in Feel. Strong in Identity
Supervisors: Klaus Hackl, Camilo Ayala Garcia

This project *Legno Veloce* ("Fast Wood") focuses on the development of a hollow bicycle frame made of ash wood. The result is an aerodynamic city bike that combines design innovation, craftsmanship, and technical precision. A distinctive feature is the free-floating saddle, which gives lightness to the structure and enhances the elegant lines of the frame. Ash wood was chosen not only for its natural aesthetic qualities but also for its mechanical properties: high elasticity and excellent vibration damping, which make it one of the most suitable materials for wooden bicycle frames. Production combined meticulous handcrafting with advanced CNC technology, enabling the realization of complex geometries with a high degree of dimensional accuracy and repeatability.

→ p. 16

Emma Boaro
ConCura: An Empowering Tool for a Gender Equal Urban Space
Supervisors: Christian Upmeier, Melani De Luca

Layla Borghi
Reimagining Workwear: Wearable Storage for Sewing Students
Supervisors: Camilo Ayala Garcia, Klaus Hackl

Setting out from the observation of gender inequalities in urban spaces, this project analyzes how cities are often organized according to male-centered models that exclude or marginalize the needs and experiences of women. Through a multidisciplinary approach that integrates feminist urban planning studies, qualitative and quantitative data, and an analysis of the local context of Bolzano/Bozen, the project investigates how fear—more than actual violence—is internalized, normalized, and limits women's freedom of movement, contributing to their exclusion from public spaces. Based on these insights, a mobile app was designed with a human-centered approach, aimed at creating a network of support and sharing among women, providing tools to report incidents, map safe places, and highlight best practices. The goal is to promote a new paradigm of active citizenship, to generate useful data for institutions, and encourage collective care for urban spaces.

Tailors and fashion designers use a wide range of measuring and sewing tools, from yardsticks and buttonhole gauges to pins, chalk, and seam rippers, which need to be easily accessible at all times. The project developed a modular and functional set of wearable garments that allows sewing students to store and keep all their essential tools within easy reach in a single place. Through interviews, the most commonly used tools were analyzed, enabling the development of an ergonomic and practical solution that ensures full accessibility during work and provides an alternative to traditional sewing boxes or cabinets. The central concept involved creating wearable accessories adaptable to different body types and sizes, following a "one-size-fits-all" approach. The collection includes a leg pouch, a chest rig, a thumbless glove, and a functional hat, all designed to avoid discomfort whether the user is standing or sitting while sewing. Special attention was given to left-handed users: by rotating or flipping the accessory, tools become equally accessible on the opposite side.

→ p. 38

→ p. 17

Tino-Roberto Bors
Alt Sibiu 1989
Supervisors: Davide Tommaso Ferrando,
Marcello Barison

Ines Brandt
*Ich Hure: Sexarbeit in Medien
und Populärkultur*
Supervisors: Andreas Trenker, Ingrid Kofler

Alt Sibiu 1989 ("Another Sibiu 1989") is an installation showing a first-person videogame set in an alternative, abstract version of the city of Sibiu, Romania. The video game foregrounds a fictitious protest situation, remixing and taking inspiration from direct and indirect accounts of people who lived through the Romanian Revolution and participated in the 1989 protest uprisings in Timişoara, Bucharest, and Sibiu, against the communist regime of Nicolae Ceauşescu. The game allows the player/spectator to wander through a maze of surfaces that follows the layout of the city of Sibiu, which gradually begins to become increasingly crowded with civilians, protesters, revolutionaries, military and law enforcement officers. In the tradition of the survival subgenre that developed after the fall of communism in Eastern Europe, the player's objective is to survive. Even though the game is not an accurate historical summary of the Romanian Revolution, the player is accompanied during the gameplay experience by testimonies and accounts of the time.

The debate on prostitution remains a central topic in social discourse, raising fundamental questions about the representation of women, self-determination, and exploitation. Although sexual services are offered daily worldwide, the topic remains a sensitive taboo, one often marked by sensationalism. In particular, the visual representation of women in the media plays a key role, as it shapes social perceptions of morality and sexuality, either reinforcing or challenging stereotypes associated with sex work. The project *Ich Hure: Sexarbeit in Medien und Populärkultur* ("I, Whore: Sex Work in the Media and Popular Culture") first examines how prostitution is represented in visual communication and then explores how these representations influence social discourse on the topic. It aims to highlight how visual language can convey the complex tensions between empowerment and stigmatization, questioning stereotypical depictions of women in prostitution and opening up new perspectives on the issue.

→ p. 76

→ p. 22

Sara Brucato
Walking On Eggshells
Supervisors: Eva Leitolf, Livia Taverna

Adrià Cano López
Spora: A participatory tool for co-creating desirable rural futures with youth
Supervisors: Sónia Cabral Matos, Teresa Palmieri

In 2024, the Italian government allocated ten million euro for psychological assistance. The response was overwhelming: 175,000 requests arrived in just two days, highlighting the urgent need for support. Yet only 11% of these requests were met due to limited funds. With the public health system burdened by long waiting lists, those with higher incomes can access private therapy, while lower-income individuals are left without care. Having personally experienced mental health difficulties without access to professional support, the artist turned to psychological themes in search of understanding. *Walking On Eggshells* explores the impact of childhood on adult life, focusing on the constant need for control borne from the fear that one's environment might suddenly inflict emotional distress. The audiovisual installation conveys this tension: the audio evokes imminent danger, while the visuals show no concrete threat—reflecting a way of living under the weight of anticipating harm that may never come.

In recent decades, rural areas across Europe have faced growing challenges, depopulation, aging communities, and shrinking services, all of which threaten not only their vitality but also broader goals of social and environmental sustainability. Despite numerous policy efforts, challenges like the brain drain and demographic imbalance remain unresolved. The project *Spora* explores how rural youth can become active agents in shaping the future of their territories. Rooted in the Appreciative Inquiry methodology and informed by the principles of place-based development, it introduces *Spora*, a participatory tool and workshop format designed to foster imagination, dialogue, and co-creation. Rather than focusing on what is missing, *Spora* begins with local strengths, inviting young participants to envision desirable futures and develop concrete, context-sensitive actions for territorial regeneration. Through this lens, the project seeks to reframe rural areas not as spaces of decline, but as fertile grounds for innovation, collaboration, and sustainable transformation, led by the very people who will inhabit them tomorrow.

→ p. 63

→ p. 92

Francesca Cantele
Spettri: An Interactive Guide Toward the Consciousness of Sound Through Listening and the Discovery of the Auditory Phenomena
Supervisors: Marc Allen Herbst, Hannes Hoelzl

This research explores the physical, perceptual, and political dimensions of sound and listening, presenting the latter not only as a conscious sensory act but also as a cultural and political choice. Listening was understood not as passive reception, but as an intentional and transformative practice, and through the study of acoustics, capable of questioning hierarchies, revealing power structures, and opening up new forms of connection with the environment and with others. This investigation culminated in *Spettri* ("Specters"), a sound installation conceived as an experimental sound system: nine speakers and an oscilloscope fragmented a single sonic signal into the frequency bands that it is made up of. The audience was invited to approach, engage, and enter a dialogue of discovery with the sound and its nature.

→ p. 77

Lisa Caprara
Songs from the Depths of Hell: La musica liberata dai campi di concentramento
Supervisors: Marcello Barison, Andrea Facchetti

Between 1933 and 1945, Nazi Germany and its allies created more than forty thousand sites of persecution—including ghettos, concentration, and extermination camps—designed to isolate, exploit, and annihilate those they defined as "enemies" of the state. In these places of forced labor, death, and extermination, prisoners created a vast body of music as a means of escaping the harsh reality they were forced to endure. The songs born in these contexts testify both to the hope of survival and to the inhuman conditions in which the prisoners lived. One of the most significant collections is *Songs from the Depths of Hell*: an album by Aleksander Kulisiewicz released in 1979, gathering fifteen songs composed in German concentration camps between 1936 and 1945. The homonymous project *Songs from the Depths of Hell* ("Music Freed from Concentration Camps") consists of a publication that uncovers the hidden stories behind these compositions, complemented by an online platform where users can listen to the album alongside the lyrics. The interplay between print and digital media creates an immersive experience that brings to light this lesser-known take on history.

→ p. 52

Alessia Maria Concetta Carbonara
Forest Bodies

Supervisors: Luca Trevisani, Marcello Barison

Forest Bodies is a series of thirteen black-and-white photographs depicting bodies composed of heterogeneous organic matter—roots, soil, moss, herbaceous plants, branches, and leaves—that take on anthropomorphic, zoomorphic, and totemic forms. These "bodies" are tree roots brought to the surface by biological processes and atmospheric phenomena, such as windthrows or the collapse of dead trees. Among the events that contributed to their formation was the Vaia Storm of 2018, which profoundly transformed the mountainous landscape of northeastern Italy, giving rise to these clusters of matter. These formations, spontaneous and metamorphic manifestations of life, challenge the conventions of biological taxonomy, assuming monstrous, architectural, animalistic, and humanoid shapes defined through the human gaze, revealing a hybridization between nature and culture. Through the series, *Forest Bodies* become an expression of matter in transformation, of the relationship between meteorological events and visual imagination, and of nature's capacity to generate archetypal forms that question the separation between humans and the natural world.

Beatrice Carner
Tracce di Memoria

Supervisors: Gerhard Glüher, Hannes Egger

The project *Tracce di Memoria* ("Traces of Memory") stems from collaboration between an emerging artist and five elderly residents of a nursing home. Drawing serves as the bridge through which their life experiences are captured and transformed into permanent visual works. The elderly, custodians of often undocumented stories and traditions, see their memories preserved and shared, while the artist interprets them through their own perception and emotions, creating a unique visual archive. The illustrations allow the audience to identify with these experiences and reflect on the meaning of life during a stage often overlooked by society. Beyond the artworks produced, the project leaves a legacy of the intergenerational bond it created, transmitting memories and stories from one generation to the next.

→ p. 67

→ p. 82

Arianna Casarin
Ninin, il ricordo dell'acqua
Supervisors: Elisabetta Rattalino, Andrea Facchetti

Inspired by the diaries of her maternal grandparents, written between 1941 and 1958, the project *Ninin, il ricordo dell'acqua* ("Ninin, the Memory of Water") investigates personal and frequently overlooked histories of Como. Following the chronology of the diaries, it focuses particularly on the period of the Second World War and its immediate aftermath. Lake Como, widely known for its beauty, was the site of significant historical events during these years, including the capture of Mussolini. The research weaves together historical narratives and personal memories. The private diaries, with their intimate reflections, offer insight into the human dimension of the official historical record. The work, realized as an editorial project, establishes connections between her grandparents' memoirs and historical documents, past and present photographs, interviews, and both direct and indirect testimonies.

Filippo Ciriani
Sonic Fractals: Listening to Venice's Housing Crisis
Supervisors: Elisabeth Tauber, Eva Leitolf

Sonic Fractals: Listening to Venice's Housing Crisis aims to explore how sound and listening practices can be used both as a tool to investigate the housing crisis and as a medium for political engagement. Building on "Solo Transitori"—a campaign focused on Venice's housing crisis developed by We Are Here Venice and OCIO—sound serves as the compass with which to investigate Venice's shifting landscape and complexity, where field recordings, soundwalks, and active listening play a political role, revealing the dynamics of urban life. While the rapid increase in property prices and the rise of short-term rentals have exacerbated housing accessibility for Venetians, this project seeks to delve into the political potential of listening as an eco-social practice capable of mobilizing collective agency.

→ p. 59

→ pp. 108–109

Angela Colapaoli
*centoottantametriquadri
("One Hundred and
Eighty Square Meters")*

Supervisors: Luca Trevisani, Marcello Barison

The processing of trauma through a repetitive, physical gesture: washing the site of pain with saliva. The transfer of 180 square meters, symbolizing the suffering experienced, from the private to the public sphere highlights the conflict between the need for purification and emotional contamination. A body, worn down and consumed by the repeated act, becomes a vehicle of anger. The use of saliva and the repetition of the gesture delve into the relationship between body and trauma, exploring the concepts of cleanliness and futility, care and exertion.

Laïsa Sophie Cordes
*Val di Torba: Creating a Space for
Agonistic Dialogue on the Future of
Peat Areas in South Tyrol*

Supervisors: Teresa Palmieri, Stefan Zerbe

Few people know that the Adige Valley in South Tyrol, now famous for its apple production, was once covered by extensive peatlands. These lands were drained in the past, and peat was extracted for decades, leading to ongoing tensions between economic and ecological interests involving residents, biologists, environmental activists, farmers, and politicians. With growing concerns over CO_2 emissions, peat extraction is now set to be banned as old licenses expire, raising the question of how to manage these areas, some of which still contain peat soil. *Val di Torba* ("Peat Valley") addresses this challenge by introducing design as a mediating discipline between different stakeholders and perspectives. Through interviews and field research, the project generated comprehensive visual material—including illustrations, animations, and future scenarios—which culminated in a participatory exhibition. The exhibition not only informed the public about peat and its extraction but also fostered a constructive dialogue among stakeholders, exploring sustainable futures for the peatlands of South Tyrol.

→ p. 32

→ p. 86

Chiara Cunoci
Spedizione Paiolo
Supervisors: Elisabetta Rattalino, Jonathan Pierini

In the southern part of Mantua, in addition to the Upper, Middle, and Lower lakes, there once stood Lake Paiolo, reclaimed in the eighteenth century and later drained and forested with trees during the Napoleonic era. Planted for military purposes, these trees shaped an ecosystem with a strong arboreal character. Today, the Paiolo Valley appears pristine and timeless, although recently threatened by urban development. From this awareness emerged *Spedizione Paiolo* ("Paiolo Expedition"): a project designed to involve the community in rediscovering the former Lake Paiolo. During three events between December 2024 and February 2025, participants explored the history and ecological value of the area through walks led by local experts. Each day produced a symbolic artefact—a map, a flag, and a raft—which together form a symbolic journey. The project resulted in a publication serving as a "travel log" to document the stories behind each artefact. Made up of three volumes featuring routes, interviews with guides, and participants' impressions, it offers multiple perspectives on the Paiolo Valley.

Allegra D'Achille
Mira: Targeted Heating for Personal Comfort
Supervisors: Nitzan Cohen, Klaus Hackl

Porcelain is reframed in this project as a localized domestic heating solution in combination with infrared technology, removing it from its traditional tableware and decorative context. The design exploits porcelain's ability to retain, distribute, and emit heat effectively, reducing the overall energy demand of the device. Unlike convection heating, which warms the air, infrared technology transfers warmth directly to objects and people thanks to radiant heat. This project explores the potential of localized, electricity-based heating by generating small heat zones within occupied spaces, enhancing efficiency, comfort, and safety. Furthermore, this design offsets the downsides of common localized portable heaters, such as overheating-related fire hazards, accidental burns and the circulation of allergens, providing a safer option overall.

→ pp. 36–37

→ p. 11

Loris Dadda
La Versatile: Adaptability of a rectangular container, the suitcase

Supervisors: Klaus Hackl, Camilo Ayala Garcia

Although our way of travelling and our approach to travel have evolved and continue to change over the decades, the most iconic item in this field, the suitcase, has remained largely unchanged in its concept, despite significant technological advancements. It is simply a container transported from point to point, filled with clothes and various other items. But have we ever questioned whether it works as effectively as it could, or considered ways to improve it? *La Versatile* ("The Versatile") is a suitcase concept that offers greater adaptability than the standard rectangular container, taking in consideration that more and more people, especially the younger generations, are travelling more frequently and often on shorter trips. The suitcase is typically a mass-produced, standard, and static product. *La Versatile, from its perspective,* is not conceived anymore as a single body, but rather of two distinct parts: a soft and a hard component. This combination allows for better management of volume and weight, with the added flexibility of using the soft part as a backpack or bag.

Diletta Maria Dell'Utri
Teaching Algorithmic Visual Design: Creative Coding and AI in Visual Design Education

Supervisors: Antonino Benincasa, Rocco Lorenzo Modugno

The project explored integrating creative coding and AI-driven generative approaches in design education, aiming to expand students' creative workflows while strengthening technical skills and critical engagement with AI outputs. Although creative coding has long existed in niche design communities, modern languages, libraries, and AI make it increasingly accessible, allowing designers to go beyond traditional software and focus on tailored tools. A central concern is the risk of overreliance on AI without technical understanding. A five-day workshop involved over 100 high-school students, with eight hours of instruction on algorithmic concepts, basic machine learning, AI-assisted coding with p5.js, and prompt engineering with Large Language Models. While AI can enhance creative workflows, its effective and responsible use depends on digital literacy, language proficiency, and active engagement, alongside algorithmic thinking and technical understanding.

→ pp. 18–19

→ p. 57

Maria del Rosario Castro Zamorano
Not Just a Piece of Paper
Supervisors: Kris Krois, Sónia Cabral Matos

Irene Delvai
The Sheep, the Island and Us
Supervisors: Elisabeth Tauber, Maria del Rosario Talevi

What does it mean to be "welcomed" into a system that makes you wait, doubt, and disappear? Focusing on the *permesso di soggiorno* (residence permit) process faced by non-EU international students in Italy, *Not Just a Piece of Paper* exposes the gap between the promise of internationalization and the reality of navigating opaque, slow, and often dehumanizing bureaucracy. Grounded in the context of the Free University of Bozen-Bolzano (unibz), this research brings together critical migration theory, design activism, and participatory methods to bring to the surface stories that often go unheard. It challenges the idea that institutions are neutral hosts—showing instead how they can become complicit in reproducing legal precarity, even as they promote a global image. Through a series of interconnected proposals, the project turns lived experience into shared, visible critique. Rather than offering a fixed solution, it uses design to highlight harm, redistribute voice, imagine alternatives, and trigger action. It argues that institutional change is not abstract—it begins with small steps, shared responsibility, and the decision to no longer look away.

The Sheep, the Island and Us aims to create a contemporary narrative around wool-related practices on the island of Sardinia, Italy, through collaborative, hands-on engagement with local artisans and young residents. The project evolved into an in-depth investigation of traditional weaving, leading to an exploration of the socio-cultural and interspecies connections surrounding Sardinian wool. To build an inclusive narrative, the project involved the younger generations, encouraging them to reconnect with the land and fostering a sense of belonging that goes beyond nationalist narratives and that challenges romanticized views of rural life. Through dialogue between young Sardinians and wool practitioners, it nurtures connections and supports sustainable practices based on care and interspecies collaboration. The project facilitates encounters and knowledge exchange, creating a contemporary narrative that highlights the cultural and ecological significance of Sardinian wool.

→ p. 93

→ p. 104

Clara Di Liberto
Fiamàzi: Storie di abitanti della Val di Fiemme, par dialèto
Supervisors: Andrea Trenker, Antonino Benincasa

Fiamàzi ("Tales of the Inhabitants of the Fiemme Valley, in Dialect") is a magazine written in the dialect of the Fiemme Valley (Trentino, northern Italy). The initiative was born with the aim of protecting the cultural and linguistic identity of the local community, countering the trend toward linguistic homogenization. The magazine, the result of in-depth linguistic, visual, and field research, embarks on a journey of rediscovering the dialect, overcoming historical prejudices that associated it with a lack of culture or lower social classes. The project explores the role of visual communication in enhancing a vernacular language, demonstrating how images and texts can integrate to deepen the understanding of local traditions. Far from being a museum artifact, *Fiamàzi* uses the dialect as a living and authentic means of communication, capable of offering new perspectives and stimulating renewed interest in a language deeply cherished by its speakers.

→ p. 49

Gaia D'Inzeo
Patti chiari, amicizia lunga: Reimagining Collaborative Housing Through Community Engagement
Supervisors: Teresa Palmieri, Marzia Bona

How can Eco-Social Design promote fair housing alternatives to the commodification of houses? *Patti chiari, amicizia lunga* ("Good fences make good friends") explores the concept of housing as a fundamental human right, challenging the current approach to housing in modern society. It delves into the housing crisis in Italy, emphasizing its systemic nature and its impact on the economy, society, and the environment. Shifting the focus from housing as a commodity to housing as a shared resource, the research highlights alternative models such as homesharing, particularly for young people and students. In cities like Bolzano, rising living costs have made housing increasingly unaffordable, creating a pressing need for creative solutions that promote independence, mobility, and social interaction. After analyzing case studies, mapping the local stakeholders and conducting ethnographic research with two host families, the project developed a prototype homesharing service in collaboration with the Alto Adige University Student Movement. A series of three workshops was organized to engage students and landlords in defining an equitable housing model that shifts away from the logic of housing as a commodity.

→ p. 100

Sarah Danièl Doetsch
Essere – Being Water: A Journey into Water Awareness
Supervisors: Seçil Uğur Yavuz, Matteo Moretti

Hannah Sophie Dusch
Equal Sphere: Feminism Workshop. Equality, Self-determination, and Justice
Supervisors: Christian Upmeier, Rosalyn Dmello

The project develops participatory strategies and personal engagement to raise public awareness of water-related issues. *Essere* ("Being") transforms complex water data into accessible and interactive experiences, offering multiple points of engagement for the audience. The methodology combines participatory data physicalization with principles of experiential learning, generating meaningful interactions that connect different areas of environmental communication and make concepts accessible and engaging, with particular attention paid to young audiences. The project unfolds through three interconnected components: an enhanced festival infrastructure at the Sete Festival (Rovereto, Trentino, Italy) that combines data visualization with sensory experiences; a children's workbook designed to guide them in exploring water awareness; and a digital platform providing information on upcoming events and open-source plans for building the installations. This integrated approach ensures continued engagement beyond the festival, fostering a sustainable dialogue on water-related issues and encouraging the active participation of young people in discussions within their families.

The project focuses on the concept of "microfeminism," examining its effects and implications within contemporary feminist discourse and its impact on young audiences. It involves the development of a participatory workshop specifically designed for middle-school students, with the goal of encouraging them to engage critically with feminist issues and to develop their own informed perspectives. The workshop is structured not only to convey knowledge about feminism, but also to foster critical thinking, reflection, and dialogue among participants. Through interactive activities, discussions, and creative exercises, students are guided to explore how feminist ideas intersect with their daily lives, social relationships, and cultural norms. The initiative emphasizes active participation, providing students with tools to identify gender inequalities and consider practical ways to promote equality and inclusivity. By combining theory with hands-on engagement, the project seeks to make feminism accessible, relevant, and inspiring for young people, encouraging curiosity, awareness, and long-term reflection on social justice and gender issues.

→ p. 103

→ p. 41

Iris Eberhardt
Der Tisch des Dorfes: A pilot project for rural development in the Allgäu
Supervisors: Kris Krois, Ingrid Kofler

Lara Farkas
Alpinesafe
Supervisors: Andreas Trenker, Ingrid Kofler

Der Tisch des Dorfes ("The Village Table") is a participatory research and design project based in a rural village in the Allgäu region of southern Germany. It explores how open inclusive spaces can support long-term strategies for resilient and future-oriented rural communities. As traditional forms of social life such as associations and volunteering decline, especially in the aftermath of the COVID-19 pandemic, the need for new models of participation becomes urgent. In response to this, *Der Tisch des Dorfes* creates a neutral and welcoming space for exchange, creativity, and collective thinking. Through interviews, surveys and a pilot event—the Feierabendhock—the project explores how participatory tools can activate local knowledge, build new connections, and empower residents to co-create visions for village life in a long-term perspective.

The project aimed to explore how graphic design could contribute to reducing risks and preventing accidents in alpine sports. It focused on improving the communication, distribution, and placement of behavioral and safety guidelines for both summer and winter alpine activities. To achieve this, risk factors in the disciplines with the highest accident rates—particularly hiking and skiing—were analyzed and incorporated into the development of the information campaign. Existing communication concepts were also studied, considering both graphic and cultural aspects, with a focus on safety and behavioral rules in alpine sports and similar contexts. Collaboration with the South Tyrolean and Austrian Alpine Clubs, mountain rescue services, hotels, tourist offices, ski resorts, and rental shops provided valuable first-hand information and data. The subsequent implementation phase reached the target audience, primarily beginners in alpine sports, who were informed in a creative and innovative way about suitable behavior, potential risks, and the consequences of unsafe practices.

→ p. 88

→ p. 42

Ludovica Faro
Bleaching Point

Supervisors: Eva Leitolf, Antonino Benincasa

This project explores an artistic practice that intertwines performance, participatory art, and narrative creation, using urban public spaces as sites of human connection and exchange. The artist contacted friends, family members, and acquaintances in various cities and countries, asking if they could host her for a few days. At each destination, she spent her time in the urban environment, carrying a bottle of bleach and a backpack of plain cotton T-shirts. The streets became the stage for her daily performance: T-shirts were bleached in public, creating opportunities for dialogue with strangers or inviting passersby to approach her. Words and reflections gathered during these encounters were then transferred onto the T-shirts using stamps and bleach, which were subsequently returned to the participants as gifts.

Laura Fedrizzi
La Traversata

Supervisors: Gianluca Seta, Marcello Barison

La Traversata ("The Crossing") is an illustrated publishing project aimed at highlighting the phenomenon and consequences of Italian emigration to Brazil through the reconstruction of a family's emigration story. Presented in a diaristic narrative form and accompanied by illustrations, it recounts the process of emigration and integration in Brazil in an intimate manner. The story begins in the early twentieth century and unfolds across generations, culminating in the author's mother's decision to leave Brazil and move to Italy to reconnect with her roots. The project thus bridges the historical phenomenon of Italian emigration with its contemporary reversal, as Italy is transformed from being a country of emigration into a destination for immigration.

→ pp. 80–81

→ p. 61

Lisa Festini Battiferro
Type & Time: A typeface design inspired by the handwriting of Vigil Raber

Supervisors: Antonino Benincasa, Ingrid Kofler

This project focuses on the design of a contemporary typeface inspired by the handwritten manuscripts of Vigil Raber, a sixteenth-century theatre director from the town of Vipiteno (South Tyrol, Italy). Raber (1490–1552) played a significant role in the city's theatrical life—not only as a director, but also as a collector and editor of numerous sacred and secular plays, which he documented by hand. The aim of the project is to develop a new typeface that combines historical reference with an independent and contemporary design approach. A selection of original manuscripts preserved in the local archive of Vipiteno serves as the foundation for this work. These documents are analyzed, contextualized, and interpreted typographically. The project explores how historical letterforms can be brought into a modern design context—not through mere replication, but through their conscious and reflective reinterpretation. By combining type design, archival research, and typographic reflection, the project thus seeks to create a typeface that stands on its own while also acting as a visual medium of cultural memory.

→ p. 50

Stefanie Fink
es Zeggale & dein Farbenkompass

Supervisors: Kuno Prey, Ingrid Kofler

The project *es Zeggale & dein Farbenkompass* ("Little present & your color compass") addresses the issue of overly heavy school bags for elementary school children. Despite school bags being ergonomically optimized today, many children still carry excessive weight on their shoulders, with possible long-term health consequences. The work begins with research into existing models, interviews with those directly involved (children, parents, and teachers), and an analysis of how school bags are packed, with particular attention to the distribution of materials inside. Based on this research, a color-coded system was proposed to simplify organization, with the goal of developing a child-friendly solution that helps reduce daily loads and protect children's health.

→ p. 28

Jana Sophie Friedrichsen
Topix: Get to Know European History Through Objects

Supervisors: Christian Upmeier, Matteo Campostrini

In recent years, crises such as the Covid pandemic, inflation, and the war of aggression in Ukraine have deeply affected younger generations. More and more often, young adults perceive current political systems as incapable of addressing challenges of this scale, and during the European elections of June 2024 it became evident that a significant portion of the youth electorate supported Eurosceptic, anti-immigration, and anti-establishment parties. Against this backdrop, the proposed project seeks to bridge the gap between European identity and the young people who represent its future through the use of symbolic objects as testimonies of the continent's history. These artifacts recount crucial moments in European history that resonate with today's political and social context. Presented through engaging visuals and accompanied by brief historical descriptions, they aim to spark young people's interest in political engagement and encourage the development of critical thinking.

Sara Gatti
Bunterschurz

Supervisors: Matteo Campostrini, Joseph Imorde

The "Blauer Schurz" is the traditional blue apron of South Tyrol, historically worn by men in agricultural and craft work. Over time, it has evolved from a practical garment into an icon of South Tyrolean culture, spreading beyond its rural roots. Widely marketed in tourism—which has at times weakened its connection to its original heritage—the apron has been reinterpreted in ways that sometimes verge on kitsch or exclusion. The *bunterschurz* ("Colorful Apron") project aims to reconnect this traditional symbol with the present by developing a contemporary version that respects the apron's origins while reflecting modern values. Through the recontextualization of the Blauer Schurz, the project promotes inclusion and respect, exploring how traditional icons can evolve without losing their cultural essence. The updated version encourages a fresh perspective on tradition, offering an apron that symbolizes the balance between cultural heritage and social progress.

→ p. 33

→ p. 20

Iraitz Gerriko Mujika
InLoops: Making returns visible

Supervisors: Camilo Ayala Garcia, Florian Dusini

The project arises from the need to rethink the value of defective returns within the production and commercial cycle. Instead of treating products with minor, non-functional defects as waste, these items are redefined and reintegrated through a circular approach. By designing a system that monitors and manages returns more effectively, the goal is to prevent these products from ending up in landfills, extending their lifecycle and reducing environmental impact. The proposed system rethinks the entire returns process, connecting internal stakeholders and external customers through a comprehensive digital application. This platform provides clear guidelines for decision-making in the triage and end-of-life management of returned products. By facilitating informed choices and implementing circular strategies, the system maximizes the utility, value, and lifespan of items with minor defects. In this way, the project challenges the traditional view of returns, transforming them into concrete opportunities for sustainability and waste reduction throughout the entire product lifecycle.

Ismaele Gregori
Re-Gazelle

Supervisors: Kuno Prey, Elisa Testori

This project explores the cultural and aesthetic value of change and adaptation in products over time, emphasizing imperfection and repair rather than concealment. It focuses on transforming an Adidas Gazelle at the end of its life into a comfortable indoor slipper, maintaining the emotional bond between the object and its user. The project provides shoemakers with specific instructions and tools to carry out this transformation as a service in their workshops. These tools include a cutting template for uniform shaping, lace tags, a leather strip to refine and close the cut, and a felt insole. Shoemakers also have the option of resoling the shoe with rubber if needed. In addition, the project develops graphic design elements to communicate the service offered by the workshop. By giving the shoe a second life, the work not only extends the product's usability but also encourages engagement with artisan workshops, promoting and enhancing the value of traditional craftsmanship.

→ p. 105

→ p. 12

Theresa Felicia Handig
Hallo, Ich* Menstruiere
Supervisors: Gianluca Camillini, Rosalyn Dmello

Katharina Maria Hanglberger
I'd Rather Be a Father
Supervisors: Eva Leitolf, Elisabeth Tauber

The menstrual cycle is a recurring bodily process, generally lasting between twenty-five and thirty-two days, in which each individual experiences a unique and fluctuating rhythm. While menstruation is often highlighted, it represents only one of the four phases of the cycle. This project aims to provide clear, accessible, and engaging information about the menstrual cycle to both menstruating and non-menstruating individuals, addressing a topic that has long been stigmatized or ignored. The work envisions a guide that explains each phase of the cycle, covering biological processes as well as practical advice on aligning diet, exercise, and daily routines with the body's rhythms. The project culminates in a print guide designed as an everyday object rather than a luxury item, providing practical answers and empowering menstruating individuals to engage with their cycle knowledgeably and enjoyably. Illustrated content enhances accessibility and helps demystify common misconceptions.

I'd Rather Be a Father examines the lives of young women who often feel marginalized and overlooked in society: mothers. The project explores the experience of motherhood, capturing a snapshot of young mothers and their emotions, including their love, despair, doubts, and anger. What understanding do we have of motherhood and how do young mothers reflect on this? As a childless women in my thirties and surrounded by mothers, I wanted to understand better what it means to be a mother. The topic was explored by observing a mother for a number of weeks with a video camera and holding interviews with young mothers about their experiences and understanding of motherhood, what difficulties they have and how they reflect on them. The results of the research—the video and audio recordings and my reflections on them—were integrated into an artistic project. This project gives young mothers a voice and let others hear and explore what motherhood means. It is not an ethnographic study; it is a snapshot, a collection, a documentation and interpretation of personal stories that have one thing in common: that love and despair are often closely intertwined.

→ p. 40

→ p. 69

Mahya Mohammad
Hosseinzadeh Hashemi
*Weaving Through Life: Stories
of Artisans Upholding Heritage*

Supervisors: Seçil Uğur Yavuz, Isacco Chiaf

Maja Sofia Hauke and
María Daniela Salgado Ochoa
*Towards Relational Learnings:
Plug-Ins for High School Curricula*

Supervisors: Teresa Palmieri,
Maria del Rosario Talevi

Weaving Through Life: Stories of Artisans Upholding Heritage, is a digital platform designed to empower Iranian artisans by connecting them directly to customers, ensuring fair wages and visibility. Rooted in ethical fashion and cultural preservation, the platform allows artisans to showcase their work, set their own prices, and gain financial independence. It integrates storytelling, education, and digital tools to empower artisans when navigating online markets, protecting their heritage, and sustaining their craft in a rapidly changing economy. The project responds to challenges artisans face, such as exploitation, a lack of digital literacy, and market inaccessibility, offering a sustainable, long-term solution. By bridging tradition with technology, the platform fosters a more ethical, connected, and sustainable craft economy.

This project addresses global crises through a lens that moves beyond Western, colonial, and capitalist frameworks. Situated in the South Tyrolean educational context, it integrates theoretical and field research with local curricular elements to develop practical "plug-in" proposals emphasizing emotional, experiential, and creative co-learning. These plug-ins support teachers as co-learners, fostering horizontal learning that incorporates non-Western and more-than-Western perspectives both inside and beyond the classroom. By offering concepts and examples of relational learning, the project expands the scope of traditional lessons, promoting interconnectedness and reflection. It encourages moving beyond entrenched binaries—human and nature, mind and heart, racial and biocultural hierarchies, and capitalist-colonial constructs—toward pluriversal and decolonial ways of understanding and engaging with the world. This approach cultivates educational practices that are relational, inclusive, and attentive to diverse ways of knowing and being.

→ p. 94

→ p. 96

Tessa Hinz
*Mano Dati: The Hidden Human
Labor of AI Systems*
Supervisors: Seçil Uğur Yavuz,
Maria Menendez Blanco

Sven Kammerer
*Soft Iteration: Designing
Response-ability Formats among
Museums and its Communities*
Supervisors: Maria del Rosario Talevi,
Marc Allen Herbst

AI is often perceived as an auton-omous, almost magical technology operating independently of human intervention, a narrative widely pro-moted by Silicon Valley tech giants. In reality, AI applications such as ChatGPT or Midjourney rely on mas-sive amounts of high-quality data, generated through extensive human labor. *Mano Dati* is a research proj-ect that seeks to make this hidden dimension of AI visible. Combin-ing social design practices—includ-ing ethnographic research, illustra-tion, and art—the project highlights the human effort behind AI systems, challenging the prevailing myth of its autonomy. By presenting this alterna-tive narrative, *Mano Dati* ("Manual Data Entry") engages future technol-ogists, particularly computer science students, encouraging them to move beyond purely algorithmic and math-ematical perspectives and to acknowl-edge the social and labor-intensive foundations of the technologies they work with.

The project explores how museums can build deeper and more meaning-ful relationships with their commu-nities while remaining adaptable in a rapidly changing world. Based on the concept of *soft iteration*, it adopts a dy-namic and participatory approach to foster shared responsibility and trust between institutions and the public. Developed in collaboration with Mu-seion, the contemporary art museum of Bolzano (Italy), and the Museion Art Club, the project experiments with new governance practices and tools such as open forums, an inter-active archive, and a "relational ob-ject," all designed to foster dialogue, mutual learning, and co-creation. The results highlight the power of relational accountability and contin-uous iteration, demonstrating how museums can transform traditional notions of accountability into empa-thetic, inclusive, and responsive rela-tionships attuned to societal changes.

→ p. 85   → p. 83

Beste Kilinç
Dolaptan Çıkanlar: A Virtual Closet for Collective Memory, Queer Materiality and Activism in Restrictive Settings

Supervisors: Marc Allen Herbst, Ingrid Kofler

Meaning "[Those that] Come Out of the Closet" in Turkish, *Dolaptan Çıkanlar,* addresses the lack of safe spaces for trans+ and queer voices in Türkiye, where political censorship and social conservatism limit self-expression. Rather than relying on external validation, the project emphasizes internal recognition, celebrating material practices that reflect identity, community, and resilience. Situated within the temporalities of fashion and style, these acts preserve trans+ narratives that have been censored or erased from dominant cultural memory. An interactive virtual closet is designed to display tangible artifacts such as clothing and accessories, while also illustrating processes and critical practices within visibility politics. By transforming everyday objects into narrative artifacts, the virtual closet enables an exploration of the reveals and conceals of identity and expression, offering a counter-narrative to cisnormative frameworks in the form of a digital journal.

Rosa Maja Klingholz
Im Garten der DDR

Supervisors: Giorgio Camuffo, Marcello Barison

Im Garten der DDR ("In the Garden of the GDR") is an illustrated book that tells the story of a family in East Germany after applying for an exit visa. The narrative, told from the perspective of a child protagonist, places a strong emphasis on emotional experiences. Based on the personal accounts of the author's mother, who lived through this period firsthand, the project artistically explores the everyday challenges and emotional burdens associated with such a decision. The book combines storytelling with explanatory texts that clarify historical and social concepts, allowing readers without prior knowledge of the GDR to understand the events and context.

→ p. 106

→ p. 62

Federica Kozma
Archivio Brianza:
Beyond the Stereotype
Supervisors: Gianluca Camillini, Roberto Gigliotti

This project explores the theme of Brianza, an area located in the northern part of Lombardy, a region in Italy known for its industrial economy. The work focuses on the stereotype that characterizes this area in an unequivocally negative way. The project began with a historical exploration of the territory to understand the origins of the stereotype, followed by a field investigation aimed at discovering who the people of Brianza really are, through interviews and photography. Design was used both as a tool to document the research process and to represent a rediscovered territory. The final outcome is an unfinished publication made up of seventeen booklets, each sixteen pages long; every booklet explores a layer, a person, or a place, with the ultimate goal of deconstructing the stereotype through images and voices. The publication aims to reveal a place that seems familiar but which is in fact largely unknown, conveying the broader reflection that truly understanding a territory and its people requires depth, going beyond stereotypes and appearances.

Yeva Kupchenko
Critical Gardens: Co-Creating
Knowledge With Ukrainian Land
and Kin
Supervisors: Maria del Rosario Talevi, Marc Allen Herbst

Critical Gardens investigates the role of Ukrainian gardens as commons —shared spaces where humans and more-than-humans co-create knowledge. Historically, gardens have been sites of refuge, resilience, and power struggles. In times of crisis, be it war, ecological disruption, or political change, they serve as spaces of memory, collective care, and reimagined futures. At the heart of this project is a commitment to epistemic justice, challenging whose knowledge is valued and how histories are remembered. Rooted in action research and critical pedagogy, the project engages Ukrainian youth in a co-designed learning process at an online democratic school in Kyiv. Instead of a rigid syllabus, the curriculum fosters collaboration, historical reflection, and creative engagement with gardens as living archives. Participants explore decolonial approaches to land and knowledge, reclaiming narratives often overlooked in dominant discourses, addressing themes of interspecies justice, cultural reclamation, and eco-social agency.

→ p. 39

→ p. 98

Stefano Lattuada
*Cities and Peaks: Bolzano,
the del Colle Cableway and the
Transformation of the Alps*

Supervisors: Elisabetta Rattalino, Claudia Polizzi

Sabrina Mandelli
*Presence by Absence
(veniamo dal lago)*

Supervisors: Gerhard Glüher, Hannes Egger

Since the early twentieth century, the Alps have undergone profound transformation in terms of reconceptualization, infrastructural development, and urbanization. Innovations such as funiculars, cable cars, and hydroelectric power stations have enabled access to previously inhospitable peaks, bringing new dynamism and modernity to these territories and intertwining technology with nature. Tourism and economic development have introduced urban values and imagery to high-altitude environments, leaving a lasting imprint across the Alpine arc. This project traces the history of these infrastructures and their role within the social and historical context of Bolzano and the Central Alps. Extensive archival research, including historical photographs, postcards, and documents, provides insight into how these materials contribute to narrating complex processes of infrastructuring and shaping tourists' perspective of the region. Presented as a publication, the work simultaneously recounts the history of landscape transformation and offers a contemporary reinterpretation of editorial approaches to historical narration.

Presence by Absence ("We Come from the Lake") is an archival space activated through the artist's performative intervention. She interacts with the "stracciatella" stones, cleaning and arranging them—an act that evolves from practical necessity into a ritual of care and engagement with the material. The work is accompanied by a booklet documenting the selected objects and the archive through photographs, providing a record of the research process. The installation invites viewers to reflect on cultural heritage and grief, exploring memory, absence, and the meaning we attribute to objects and stories of the past. An audio component fills the space with the artist's voice reading her grandfather's handwritten notebook, an intimate document preserving dialect words, proverbs, and stories from his time.

→ p. 46

→ p. 79

Nicola Marchiori
Fabri.Cap – Fabric Waste as an Opportunity for Self Production
Supervisors: Gianluca Camillini, Andrea Signoretto

The fashion and outdoor apparel industries generate significant amounts of pre- and post-consumer textile waste. *Fabri.Cap* investigates how outdoor brands manage textile waste; it identifies the most common sources of fabric leftover, assesses current waste-handling strategies, and explores opportunities for up-cycling. The final outcome is a collection of DIY hat-making instructions that transform leftover fabrics into functional, wearable accessories. By transforming waste into an opportunity for hands-on creation, the project aims to reconnect individuals with the products they wear, fostering a deeper awareness of responsible consumption through agency.

→ p. 13

Anna Martinatti
Pratiche di autogoverno in Trentino: Reimagining Self-Government Practices of Collective Lands Together With New Generations
Supervisors: Jacopo Ammendola, Maria del Rosario Talevi

Pratiche di autogoverno in Trentino ("Self-Governing Practices in Trentino") investigates the topic of collective lands, focusing on self-governance as a tool for local development. Trentino is an autonomous province in northern Italy, characterized by mountains, valleys, and an economy that combines agriculture, industry, and tourism. Here, collective lands—including forests, meadows, pastures, rivers, lakes, and roads—cover more than half of the territory and can be accessed, used, and managed autonomously by local residents. The project began with preliminary research in the Rotaliana, Paganella, and Bassa Val di Non areas, revealing issues in the municipal management of collective lands. Building on the experience of the association La Foresta – Accademia di comunità (Rovereto), the work followed two main strategies: raising awareness through visual materials and fostering a participatory process of rediscovery together with younger generations. Through co-design activities, the project envisions more equitable and responsible ways to (self-)govern local collective lands.

→ p. 102

Giulio Marzatico
Real Artificial Emotions
Supervisors: Giulia Cordin, Melani De Luca

The project investigates the rapid advancement of artificial intelligence and its impact on society and interpersonal relationships. In particular, the continuous refinement of AI's practical human capabilities raises questions about the risk of cultural homogenization and the reduction of individual diversity. Emotional chatbots contribute to phenomena such as "shared loneliness" and affective manipulation, with potential negative repercussions on interpersonal relationships. Furthermore, AI now attempts to simulate and understand emotions: a trend that could standardize feelings and experiences, putting their authenticity at risk. The project critically examines these issues to explore how AI could instead evolve ethically, respecting the complexity of human experience.

Ingrid Meszaros
Perceptional: Sonic Exploration of Data and Emotion
Supervisors: Davide Tommaso Ferrando, Seçil Uğur Yavuz

The project explores sonification as a method of representing data through a physical means of sound production, using biometric information. It goes beyond digital sonification by incorporating servomotors and material contact to create haptic experiences. The final installation monitored the stress of a group of students during the nine weeks leading up to their thesis submission. Biometric data—HRV and BPM—were translated into rhythmic sounds via servomotors connected to pens placed on a round metal sounding box. Stress oscillations were then transformed into sounds, while the iron surface resonated, evoking the passage of time, deadlines, and recurring sources of pressure. By using physical rather than digital sonification, the project subverts conventional data visualization. The study promotes a sensory and affective approach to information design, transforming data from passive observation into active experience and fostering new conversations about our everyday relationship with information.

→ p. 34

→ p. 7

Anna Migliorini
Msna: Minori Stranieri Non Accompagnati

Supervisors: Mustapha El Moussaoui, Rocco Lorenzo Modugno

Clara Milla
Bodies of Remembrance as Hybrid Remedies

Supervisors: Luca Trevisani, Davide Tommaso Ferrando

MSNA is the acronym for "Unaccompanied Foreign Minors." In the social work sector, the acronym is widely recognized, whereas among the general public it often sparks curiosity due to limited awareness and available information. The character created to personify this community highlights the very young individuals it represents, who themselves might not recognize the meaning of the acronym. The project is grounded in Italian legislation and builds on research conducted within the local context, aiming to provide visibility, understanding, and accessibility regarding the challenges and realities faced by unaccompanied minors. By combining design, narratives, and research, the work seeks to bridge the gap between social services, the community, and the broader public.

Bodies of Remembrance as Hybrid Remedies is a sculptural exploration rooted in a deep nostalgia for a time before humanity's separation and isolation from its environment, and ultimately, from itself. This project questions the only reality the artists lived in, guided by an inner knowing that there is more to be felt, perceived, and embodied. Through this inquiry, something both new and deeply primordial is imagined and materialized into form. Between the primordial and the yet-to-be-created, sentient bodies emerge, carrying traces of interwoven agencies. These sculptures are not static objects but extensions of a reciprocal relationship, evolving closely around the artist's body. The act of carrying them becomes an intimate gesture of interdependence, a physical dialogue between the self and material. The surfaces of these sculptures are layered with collected fibers—human hair, animal hair and fibers, plant matter, and fragments of other organic and synthetic materials—re-imagining a body that transcends individual identity into relational, hybrid forms of existence.

→ p. 60

→ p. 66

Ariana Georgiana Mirea
Totu Moare în România
Supervisors: Luca Trevisani, Eva Leitolf

This project *Totu Moare în România* ("Everything Dies in Romania") emerges from the need to explore, through artistic practice and theoretical reflection, the experience of forced migration as a fracture that runs through memory, family ties, and the body. The work takes an autoethnographic perspective, weaving together personal narratives, performance, and cultural analysis to investigate how absence, nostalgia, and longing shape the diasporic experience. At the center of the research is *pomana*, a Romanian funerary ritual reimagined as a performative gesture and act of poetic resistance. Transposed from the domestic sphere to a public space, the ritual takes on a new function: not only to commemorate, but to share and make visible the migratory rupture. The concept of *dor*, a deep emotional state of longing and loss, runs through the entire project as its affective and narrative engine. The performance proposes a symbolic alternative to private mourning, transforming it into a collective space of care and imagined reconnection. In this way, art becomes a tool to redefine belonging, to create ties in absence, and to inhabit the space between what has been lost and what may still be generated.

→ p. 68

Nicol Moalli
Elvira Storytelling: A Digital Experience amid Feminism and Reflection
Supervisors: Letizia Bollini, Andreas Trenker

The project developed a digital experience to raise awareness of the importance of feminism in the first half of the twentieth century, showing how the movement benefited society as a whole and not just women. It was carried out in two main phases: historical research and digital design. The first phase focused on the work of the Elvira Badaracco Foundation in Milan, highlighting the complete absence of male participation in events and archive consultations, and the need to engage men more actively. The second phase produced a digital narrative in the first person of Elvira Badaracco, a central figure of the feminist movement in the 1970s, structured around interactive questions on key feminist laws to stimulate reflection on their historical and social impact. The digital content was created using open-source tools, allowing the Foundation to integrate it independently into its website.

→ p. 45

Dora Musola
Il Debutto

Supervisors: Eva Leitolf, Hannes Egger

In contemporary culture, constructing a personal narrative is key to gaining visibility and success. Artists and public figures shape their image alongside their work, managing it as a personal brand. This often involves cultivating an idealized self—a version perceived as desirable and socially acceptable. Idols, influencers, and celebrities, defined by recognizable values and aesthetics, serve as models to emulate, forming the basis of celebrity culture. This project investigates the traits, history, and influence of celebrity culture on personal and collective identity. *Il Debutto* ("The Debut") explores the construction of an idealized self through personal narrative manipulation. By observing and transforming one's image, the work reflects on the self as a crafted project, interrogating the tension between authenticity and performance, and highlighting the cultural obsession with self-image and the challenges of self-fashioning.

Gianluca Norcia
Unimakers

Supervisors: Kuno Prey, Elisa Testori

Ensuring living spaces that favor the psychophysical and emotional well-being of the occupants is of fundamental importance, even in temporary contexts. This project is a practical handbook for university students moving into a new room for the first time. It intends to respond to the need for customization and optimization of spaces, providing ideas and instructions for building customized, economical and functional furniture on one's own. Starting from an analysis of the typical challenges that new students encounter—limited availability of space, a low budget and the need to create a comfortable and personal environment—the manual offers ideas and suggestions for flexible and adaptable furniture. Through explanations on materials, the use of basic tools and detailed instructions, students are guided in the creation of essential furniture items. Each project is designed to be interpreted with accessible materials and reclaimed elements.

→ pp. 72–73   → p. 23

Arthur Paul Ottmann
Nocciólo: Exploring an Undiscovered Local Resource for Furniture Construction

Supervisors: Klaus Hackl, Sónia Cabral Matos

This project explores the potential of hazelnut bushes (Corylus avellana) as a sustainable material for furniture design, overlooked by profit-driven industries. The plant is widespread in Alto Adige and offers various processing possibilities that can be applied to furniture compositions. The project includes research on the plant's local significance in terms of environmental, forestry, and traditional aspects. This is followed by practical research on how hazelnut bushes can be processed and integrated into furniture design. As a result, the *Nocciólo* ("Hazelnut Tree") project presents a series of furniture pieces that demonstrate the potential of hazelnut rods through various processing techniques. The *Nocciólo* furniture combines hazelnut rods with aluminum profiles, creating a contrast that highlights the unconventional use of naturally grown elements in furniture making.

Josef Pachmayr
CircuLarv

Supervisors: Klaus Hackl, Camilo Ayala Garcia

CircuLarv is a sustainable system that enables users to convert food waste into high-quality insect feed for pets such as reptiles, dogs, and cats, as well as for livestock like chickens and fish. The focus is on ease of use, resource efficiency, and environmental sustainability. By upcycling waste, *CircuLarv* reduces environmental impact and provides a sustainable alternative to conventional animal feed. The goal is to create a self-sustaining ecosystem that benefits both pet owners and the environment.

→ pp. 14–15

→ p. 8

Greta Papaveri
Altri paesaggi: Narrating Italian Rural Landscapes Through Co-Creation and Exploration
Supervisors: Sónia Cabral Matos, Daniele Ietri

Nicola Parise
Is It Really Our Duty to Add Fresh Ruins to the Field of Ruins?
Supervisors: Roberto Gigliotti, Davide Tommaso Ferrando

As urban crises intensify, rural areas have gained prominence in political, socio-economic, and cultural debates, giving rise to new paradigms of rurality that emphasize environmental quality, wellbeing, and a slower pace of life. *Altri paesaggi* ("Other Landscapes") explores alternative landscapes beyond dominant policy and media-driven narratives, investigating community-driven governance through collective narratives. Focusing on field research at the Val di fiastra Landscape Observatory in the Marche region and using ethnographic methods, including participant observation and interviews, the research examines how professionals and local inhabitants co-design future-oriented community narratives and the challenges posed by top-down approaches. Informed by these insights, *Altri paesaggi* proposes a reflexive, inclusive methodology to engage rural inhabitants in co-creating grassroots landscape narratives. An editorial tool supports professional in facilitating participatory rural gatherings, translating individuals' emotional and subjective connections to their environment into collective dialogues that envision futures reflecting local needs, values, and aspirations.

The project focuses on conceiving and designing an exhibition that explores the urban traces of Fascism in Bolzano, a city in northern Italy, which was forcibly Italianized during the Fascist regime in the 1930s. The exhibition centers on Siegesplatz/Piazza della Vittoria and its monumental architecture, which embodies the city's symbolic transformation during the Fascist period. The concept of the exhibition involves selecting specific urban traces of Fascism and presenting them as re-contextualized objects. The artifacts displayed are not exact replicas of what exists in the city but rather reinterpretations that invite reflection. Once brought into the exhibition space, these objects are "re-politicized," as their meaning shifts in relation to their new environment. In this context, the artifacts appear distant from the bold Fascist imagery still scattered throughout the city, often reduced to faint traces of their original presence. This approach encourages visitors to consider the contemporary significance of these historical remnants and reflect on how the memory of Fascism persists across the urban landscape.

→ p. 101

→ p. 29

Johanna Pauer and
Xavier Pettigrew
*Trephor: In it for the Long Run /
Eco-Social Transformation in
Endurance Sports Nutrition through
Design and Entrepeneurship*

Supervisors: Seçil Uğur Yavuz, Alessandro Rossi

The growing popularity of outdoor sports makes it urgent to rethink endurance sports nutrition to meet the needs of both athletes and the planet. Currently, much of sports nutrition still relies on single-use plastics and unsustainable practices. The project demonstrates how endurance sports nutrition can be redesigned to reduce dependence on plastic and facilitate access to adequate nutrition for outdoor activities. During extensive testing with endurance athletes, the proposed solution—a reusable packaging system paired with compatible semi-liquid nutrition—received excellent feedback, confirming its potential for a positive impact on the outdoor sports industry.

Severin Piller
Rigid: A Portable Seating Solution

Supervisors: Camilo Ayala Garcia, Klaus Hackl

This project explores portable seating, with a focus on folding chairs, examining their history, types, and mechanisms. Through research and testing of existing products, a solution was developed for outdoor enthusiasts, such as campers and hikers, as well as for urban or emergency contexts. The proposed chair combines safety, weather resistance, and durability with core design principles, including structural integrity, joint quality, and material selection, resulting in a versatile, functional, and innovative product.

→ p. 99

→ p. 31

Chiara Pinzan
Fragmented Echoes: The Silent
Witnesses of Murano

Supervisors: Gianluca Camillini, Roberto Gigliotti

Margherita Poli and Viola Redaelli
Non ti arrabbiare: Exploring
Dialogue in Mental Health Context

Supervisors: Sónia Cabral Matos,
Maria del Rosario Talevi

"The city is the projection of society onto the territory," and it transforms through global processes and profound shifts in production, urban-rural relationships, and social structures. Following this perspective from French sociologist Henry Lefebvre, the project examines Murano, the author's hometown. Until the twentieth century, Murano's local culture maintained a continuity centered on glass production—a phenomenon described as a glassware monoculture. The transition to a global city, however, brought significant economic and social changes, transforming Murano from primarily a production site into a predominantly commercial hub. The fragmentation and downsizing of the glass furnaces, however, has led to the erosion of artisanal knowledge and socio-cultural impoverishment. By highlighting the fragility of the island's cultural heritage, the project aims to document these societal transformations from the twentieth century to the present and how they are reflected in both the territory and its community. Through a visual communication approach, it collects fragments of Murano's identity, including lost architectural histories and first-hand testimonies from inhabitants.

While mental health institutions, particularly in Italy, have undergone significant transformations, they often continue to operate within insufficient care models. Psychiatric and healthcare systems frequently prioritize efficiency over meeting the actual needs of those they serve. Hierarchies within these institutions remain rigid, and individuals experiencing mental illness continue to face stigma and medicalization. Interviews highlighted recurring issues concerning hierarchies, power dynamics, and social roles, revealing a lack of peer-to-peer communication in psychiatric settings. *Non ti arrabbiare* ("Don't Get Angry") emerged as an eco-social design project addressing these communication challenges in mental healthcare. The project emphasizes dialogue, exchange, and collaborative problem-solving rooted in personal experience and subjective perspectives. Designed as a practical tool, *Non ti arrabbiare* transforms hierarchical interaction into opportunities for critical dialogue, cooperative problem-solving, and emancipatory practices.

→ p. 43

→ p. 95

Martina Poschiavin
Aldidanché
Supervisors: Kuno Prey, Ingrid Kofler

The project *Aldidanché* ("Nowadays") aims to reintroduce the tradition of gifting handcrafted furniture on important occasions, such as weddings or the birth of a child, drawing inspiration from the customs of the Fassa Valley in northern Italy. Located in the Dolomites, the Fassa Valley is home to the Ladin linguistic minority, known for its rich culture, traditions, art, and creativity. The result is a small pinewood casket, carved with auspicious symbols and characterized by clean, geometric lines. Equipped with a secret double bottom and internal organizers, the casket is designed to hold memories and small precious objects, combining functionality, elegance, and symbolic value.

Chiara Prosser
Incontra design
Supervisors: Klaus Hackl, Ingrid Kofler

Incontra design ("Meet Design") arises from the need to promote collaboration and inclusivity among children, creating a space for free, creative, and boundless play. In school, children often seem estranged from one another, and conflicting educational approaches make it hard to find common ground. *Incontra design* is conceived as a powerful educational tool for primary schools, offering an alternative to traditional passive and stereotypical toys, and fostering emotional and social development. The project helps children develop self-confidence and trust, face challenges beyond traditional educational limits, and cultivate empathy and cooperation. Boys and girls discover that only by joining forces can they build what they imagine. The system consists of four interchangeable elements that combine into infinite configurations through a connector, allowing children to build, explore, and reinvent play spaces. Without instructions or right or wrong outcomes, *Incontra design* adapts to each child's intuition, enabling them to create beyond themselves while trust is given without providing solutions.

→ p. 24   → p. 25

Francesca Re
*Come me, nessuno: A Story About
Self-Acceptance to Raise Awareness
of Eating Disorders*

Supervisors: Gianluca Camillini,
Anton Gionata Ferrari

Nowadays, eating disorders (ED) affect more than fifty-five million people worldwide, of which three million in Italy alone (Italian Institute of Statistics, 2023). Since the age of the onset of eating disorders has significantly decreased in recent years (Ministry of Health, 2023), there is an urgent need to implement prevention measures on this issue in order to make up for the lack of information and to educate children about it from an early age. *Come me, nessuno* ("Nobody Like Me") aims to raise awareness of the topic of EDs and to help prevent its insurgence. The project is not only aimed at children but also at their caregivers, as the family context plays a crucial role in such issues. The project consists of an illustrated story about bodily perception and self-acceptance, which can be enjoyed by both children from the age of six upwards and their parents or educators.

Grete Henriette Rederer
Aftertouch Vol. 1

Supervisors: Eva Leitolf, Shona Kitchen

Aftertouch Vol. 1 is an ambiguous title, alluding on the one hand to a musical term that describes the lingering pressure on a key after it is struck, and in an allegorical sense to the emotional echo of a sexual assault. The work consists of a three-channel video installation paired with a performative part, which explores the complex, mutated and twisted terrain of female sexual agency and pleasure. Through stroboscopic projections in a darkened space, techno music and layered spoken word, the piece creates a bizarre tension between agitated anticipation, sensory overload, and paralyzing horror. The core of the work consists of the song text: three stories, each told to the artist by women close to her—stories of sex, power dynamics, and violation. How is female sexuality shaped by internalized and external power structures? Female desire and lust seem indistinguishable from trauma, and in order to separate the two, word by word, memory by memory, they must first be critically examined and, above all, called by their name. *Aftertouch Vol. 1* is the first part of an ongoing series based on interviews and stories from countless other women.

→ p. 58

→ pp. 64–65

Koenraad Gerardus Reerink
*Plot Twist: How to start an
Eco-Social Farm*
Supervisors: Elisabeth Tauber, Kris Krois

Hannah Viktoria Richter
*Olympia München 1972:
Design in Dialogue*
Supervisors: Mustapha El Moussaoui, Martin Fengel

In an era dominated by industrial agriculture, *Plot Twist* explores how small-scale farming can foster social innovation, ecological resilience, and economic sustainability. Focusing on Wiesl Hof in South Tyrol as a living laboratory, the project investigates farming practices that prioritize community engagement, shared governance, and alternative market models. Using ethnographic research, case studies, and participatory action research, it examines young farmers' main challenges: land access, financial viability, and social integration. Design methodologies are applied to prototype new models of social farming, direct market strategies, and cultural programs, showing how farms can cultivate not only food but also relationships, knowledge, and collective work. By bridging research and practice, *Plot Twist* positions small-scale farming as more than a business—it becomes a common resource and a catalyst for social change, offering models for sustainable, community-oriented food systems.

The 1972 Olympic Games in Munich aimed to present a new image of Germany after WWII. The focus was on openness, modernity, and a democratic self-concept. These values were consistently reflected in architecture, graphic design, and landscape planning, which were carefully coordinated to communicate such principles. The Olympic Park, with its flowing landscape, transparent architecture, and cohesive visual concept, set new design standards. The 1972 Olympics demonstrated that design functions not only as an aesthetic tool but also as a social one, fostering community and creating spaces that bring people together. Design decisions extended beyond mere functionality, actively contributing to the creation of identity and atmosphere. Conversations with designers, contemporary witnesses, and visitors reveal how these concepts influence perceptions of the Olympic Park today. The project is recounted in a publication that documents the historical design of the Olympic Park while exploring how its principles can be reinterpreted in a contemporary context.

→ p. 87

→ p. 51

Anton Sisa Don Ropers
Flightgeist
Supervisors: Klaus Hackl, Aart van Bezooijen

Flightgeist is a hybrid paragliding and lifestyle cockpit bag designed to help young pilots enjoy this growing alpine sport safely and practically. Paragliders often face the challenge of carrying numerous small items—such as variometers, gloves, helmets, sunglasses, ski masks, and drop weights for tree rescues—that do not fit well in highly engineered backpacks or harnesses. *Flightgeist* is made of durable nylon and is suitable for everyday use, while also serving a functional purpose during flight. fiberglass tent poles can be inserted to rigidify the bag, which can then be attached to the pilot's main carabiners. This setup allows the pilot to secure instruments such as the variometer and GPS to the bag over their legs while seated, providing a stable, convenient cockpit panel during flight.

Carlotta Rudari
Rivelare le rovine: Uno spazio tra luce e silenzio nel paesaggio di Piagù
Supervisors: Ofer Kristal, Sónia Cabral Matos

In contemporary society, the need to reconnect with nature is ever more urgent. The project *Rivelare le rovine: Uno spazio tra luce e silenzio nel paesaggio di Piagù* ("Revealing Ruins: A Space Between Light and Silence in the Landscape of Piagù") proposes an immersive structure, a place of contemplation that promotes mindfulness through silence and natural light, and deepens the relationship with the landscape. Inserted in a ruin in Piagù, on Mount Baldo (Northern Italy), the installation invites contemplation and reflection, stimulating a deep sensory experience. The intervention develops in the respect of the existing tower, appreciating the imperfection and charm of the ruin and creating a memory connection between past and present. Through the use of local materials and a minimalist approach, the project dialogues with the surrounding environment, revealing the *genius loci* and offering a space for spiritual connection by valorizing the biodiversity of the landscape.

→ p. 10

→ p. 30

Lea Alina Särchinger
Bellevue di Monaco: Städtischer Widerstand im Glockenbachviertel, München ("Urban Resistance in the Glockenbachviertel, Munich")
Supervisors: Roberto Gigliotti, Matteo Compostrini

Urban development, particularly in the form of gentrification, often generates resistance due to issues of economic justice and the transformation of public space. This project examines these dynamics through the case of Bellevue di Monaco: a residential and cultural center in the heart of Munich. Originating from a citizen protest against municipal demolition plans, Bellevue has evolved since its founding in 2015 into a vital institution within the city, offering housing and support services to a diverse population, including refugees seeking language courses, counseling, and cultural programs. The project documents the development of this space over the years, highlighting the people and events that shaped it. The research culminates in a set of six interconnected books, each addressing a distinct aspect of the center. Combining texts, photographs, interviews, and sound, the work creates a multifaceted portrayal of Bellevue di Monaco, offering readers an immersive understanding of its social, cultural, and spatial significance.

Katharina Mercedes
Alexandra Schwab
Greet the Grief: Individual Recovery Through Artisanal Forms of Personal and Shared Grieving
Supervisors: Klaus Hackl, Gerhard Glüher

Greet the Grief is a social design project that supports bereaved people through the stages of grief, encouraging creative expression and reflection on personal emotions. The project is based on the finnish Ryijy technique: a manual knotting process for rugs, whose slow and structured workflow promotes relaxation, reflection, and a sense of control. The product includes an educational handbook, divided into three leporellos, and a personalized kit with materials to create one's own rug. Through this approach, *Greet the Grief* fosters a creative and therapeutic journey, transforming the grieving process into an active, reflective, and shared experience.

→ p. 47 → p. 21

Emanuele Signorini
Tempo Giusto:
A Universal Bike Rack
Supervisors: Klaus Hackl, Camilo Ayala García

Viola Silvi
Crossing These Times
Supervisors: Marc Allen Herbst, Leander Schwazer

The debate on urban livability has become heated in recent years, increasingly with a view to returning the city to its citizens. With this in mind, various urban plans have emerged that aim to split large cities into many micro realities, where city life can establish a community and strong ties, as well as live in a more sustainable and healthy way. In this new urban vision, the bicycle becomes a very valuable element to experience the city at its best and to be able to move around within it. This is why the new European plans aim to create new cycle paths and to encourage citizens to exploit this means of transport. It is in this scenario that *Tempo Giusto* ("Right Time") was born: a frontal rack capable of adapting to cyclists' various needs and accompanying them throughout their urban transit. This rack is designed to be universal and easily shared between users.

Over the course of five months, ten selected online news stories were given physical form through the practice of cross-stitching, a kind of embroidery. This ancient practice composes images by creating about 3 mm X-shaped stitches on fabric by hand with a threaded needle. This detailed succession of individual stitches requires a considerable amount of time to complete the representation of the whole subject chosen. Because of the slowness of this procedure, copying the headlines and images of the constantly updating and volatile news means embarking in an impossible task, leading to a series of pieces inevitably being left incomplete. The methodical work of cross-stitching dynamically mirrors the experience of reading the news every day and seeing it constantly change. The way many events occur simultaneously leaves the sense that many unresolved issues are left behind, and that the only option is to just move one's attention down the line.

→ p. 9

→ p. 75

Mattia Sottoriva
Tracks of Change

Supervisors: Christian Upmeier, Markus Schlaffke

In the context of the railway connection project between Verona and Padua, commonly known as TAV, Vicenza finds itself at the center of a radical transformation of its social landscape. In particular, the project to connect Vicenza with the nearby city of Padua will lead to the removal and cementification of two major green areas: the Bosco Lanerossi and the Ca' Alte forest. Over the years, these natural spaces have contributed to the creation of a small yet vital ecosystem that supports local wildlife and provides oxygen to a city like Vicenza, one of the most polluted in Italy. Additionally, the Bocciodromo, a key gathering place for Vicenza's alternative culture scene, is earmarked for demolition to make way for new roads, construction sites, and luxury apartments. Through a documentary film, this project aims to document the impact of these changes on local areas. It seeks to capture the current state of these places through on-site research and study while critically analyzing the environmental and social consequences associated with these large-scale infrastructure projects.

→ p. 35

Veronika Vascotto
Selfphone: Identity in the Smartphone Era

Supervisors: Maria del Rosario Talevi, Melani De Luca

This research investigates the complex relationships people develop with their smartphones. Starting from a philosophical analysis of the device, the study draws on neurological and psychological research to understand the mechanisms behind smartphone attachment, which, although not yet officially classified as an addiction in the DSM, clearly influences daily behavior. Using Jean M. Twenge's insights on generational differences, the research explores how individuals from different technological eras relate to their smartphones. Data was collected through structured, semi-structured, and open interviews, questionnaires, and artistic interventions. Artistic outputs communicate these findings in an engaging and interactive manner, encouraging reflection and dialogue among participants. Workshops were also developed, providing participants with structured exercises to observe and critically engage with their own smartphone use. Participant feedback was collected to assess the clarity and impact of the artistic medium while contributing additional qualitative data.

→ p. 107

Beatrice Venturato
*(Barely) Private Matters:
Examining the History
of Gossip in the Tabloid Press*
Supervisors: Gianluca Seta, Marcello Barison

Since its origins, celebrity news and gossip have played a central role in media culture, both influencing and adapting to social and technological changes. From the first illustrated magazines of the nineteenth century to the glossy magazines of the twentieth century, the way of narrating and consuming lifestyle news has profoundly transformed. This project aims to analyze the evolution of celebrity journalism in three different eras—the United States during the 1920s and 1930s, Italy during the economic boom of the 1950s and 1960s, and the United Kingdom in the 1980s and 1990s—through the lens of graphic and communicative language. The study of the evolution of the gossip genre is thus contextualized alongside the development of media and publishing. The project is not a historical reconstruction, but a design-based reflection on how gossip emerges and how it shapes the collective imagination.

Jonas Vogt
*Commonhood: Enacting Commons
through Convivial Technologies*
Supervisors: Teresa Palmieri, Kris Krois

Commonhood is a digital prototype and design research project that asks: What kind of technology could support the slow, situated labor of communing, rather than extracting, accelerating, or automating it? Rooted in a feminist, post-capitalist design lens, *Commonhood* emerges as a convivial web platform that helps collectives map what they can offer and what they need—not to commodify, but to connect. Offers and needs become relational gestures. The platform suggests potential matches between them while intentionally limiting features: no messaging, no automation, no metrics. Just space to notice, respond, and reciprocate. Rather than scaling or optimizing exchange, the platform invites collective experimentation: how can we provision together differently? Developed through co-design with real collectives, *Commonhood* is both tool and inquiry. It explores how design might shift from making products to enabling relationships, and how technology can become an ally in building plural, situated, and interconnected commons.

→ p. 54

→ p. 91

Lea Vrabelova
Street Photo Festival Napoli
Supervisors: Andreas Trenker, Gerhard Glüher

The project presents the creation of a visual identity for a new annual street photography festival, set to debut in Naples in September 2026. Initially conceived as a client-based assignment, the project evolved into an independent design proposal, expanding beyond its original conceptual constraints. It envisions a fully developed festival, including organizational structure, core values, a provisional program, and selected locations. The final outcome encompasses a comprehensive visual identity and communication materials across print, web, and social media, drawing inspiration from urban street signage and integrating it with the aesthetics of street photography. By merging the language of the city with the visual culture of photography, the project establishes a distinctive and coherent identity, reflecting the festival's dynamic and contemporary spirit.

Antonia Carola Werkmüller
Inbetween: In Conversation with Brands
Supervisors: Christian Upmeier, Rocco Lorenzo Modugno

Fashion has always been a form of self-expression—not just for the customer, but for the brand itself. How does a brand shape its identity, connect with its audience, and define success while facing challenges to its longevity? Through interviews with eight designers, founders, and creative visionaries, this project explores the process of building a fashion brand, examining strategies in branding, audience engagement, and market positioning. The resulting book delves into the ambitions, struggles, and philosophies that shape contemporary fashion, offering a unique perspective on both thriving brands and those that were unable to maintain their place in the industry. Rather than offering a formula for success, it allows readers to recognize patterns, draw connections, and reflect on the decisions that shape a brand's trajectory.

→ p. 55   → p. 44

Nina Wittenbrink
Labor Spheres: Creating con fusion
Supervisors: Teresa Palmeri, Andrea Fumagalli

This project investigates alternative labor practices through the lens of democratic participation within social cooperatives, with a focus on Bolzano, Italy. A key outcome of the research is the development of the "Spheres" tool: an interactive framework designed to visualize and enhance democratic processes in labor organizations. The tool emphasizes inclusive practices, addressing aspects such as decision-making, communication, and ownership, and provides a practical approach for fostering participation within cooperative work environments. By applying eco-social design principles, the work offers actionable strategies to promote workplace democratization and more human-centered labor practices.

→ p. 97

Nitzan Cohen
When Words Fail:
A Reflection

There is a deeply personal and quietly radical moment when each art and design graduate crosses the threshold of completion: that of the final review, the closing line, the shot captured, the form rendered, the act performed, the matter printed, or the structure built. These moments, small yet seismic, mark the end of a long process of exploration, doubt, and decision. They signal not only academic achievement, but the emergence of a professional identity shaped through personality and practice.

When Words Fail reflects on the boundaries of language and the expressive potential that emerges when those boundaries are breached. In life, it is often when language falls short that art and design intervene in their own uncontainable ways, when we feel, see, hear, and sense all the more intensely through form, image, sound, gesture, and material. Here, "failure" is not the opposite of success but a necessary step in the creative process, opening up space for discovery, redefinition, and renewal.

This takes on new urgency as artificial intelligence and machine learning increasingly shape how we communicate, represent, and interpret the world. These systems thrive on pattern and predictability, yet art and design flourish in what escapes them: the opaque, the intuitive, the ambiguous, and the unpredictable. When words fail, artistic forms engage with what resists reduction to code, generating meaning through material, movement, intuition, and atmosphere. This is not opposition, but the affirmation of another dimension: one which is fluid, inconsistent, emotional, and unmistakably human.

Our faculty—interdisciplinary, international, and rooted in South Tyrol's complex cultural landscape—nurtures this dimension daily. Students work through making: tactile materials, intentional gestures, expressive forms that speak where language cannot. Grounded in iteration and embodied experience, making becomes both method and necessity, a way to think through the body and act in the world.

The works in this volume reflect this engagement: some quiet, some bold, all attuned to the urgencies of the present. Together, ninety-five thesis projects developed between 2024 and 2025 enter into dialogue, each offering a proposition: to repair, to resist, to renew, to reimagine social fabrics, to reclaim overlooked narratives, to go against the grain and propose new rhythms of coexistence and care.

We are living through times that demand more than polished narratives or universal truths, for these are times that call for deepening, not flattening. Certainty can feel reassuring, but it often steamrolls what is nuanced, emerging or becoming. At their most alive and essential, design and art open up space for contradiction, friction, and multiplicity. They welcome questions that cannot be answered and meanings that shift with context. Here, ambiguity is not a flaw but a force, where doubt becomes method and intuition inquiry.

Diplorama! is more than a graduation celebration: it is a snapshot of a living institution, one that interrogates disciplinary norms rather than reproducing them. It is a site of exchange between art and design, between theory and practice, and between local specificity and global discourse.

At the edge of language, when words really do fail, failure becomes an opening: one in which visual, spatial, material, and sonic forms may unfold and resonate. New grammars emerge from intuition, rupture, and response. The young artists and designers whose works fill these pages do not simply speak; they shape and unshape, sense and unsettle. Their work may not always translate, but it resonates, provoking reflection, conversation, and further action.

Look at these works as a living record of inquiry —speculative, critical, and tender in their transformations. Let us celebrate not only the current peaks of these journeys but the futures they set in motion: futures shaped by care, curiosity, and the courage to begin anew. Futures where, when words fail, other languages emerge, ones of form, friction, gesture, and silence.

As we stand at this threshold between education and application, between intention and impact, we can ask what bold gestures, unlikely alliances, and imaginative practices might we now ignite? How might they transform not only how we create, but how we live together, teach one another, and generate meaning in times of urgency? What futures can we craft with our hands, our voices, and our doubts? And what making practices might yet catalyze those worlds we can no longer afford to postpone?

Giulia Cordin
When Words Are Not Enough: Reclaiming Practice-Based Knowledge Production

First presented in 2009 as a research poster during a conference in Florida, ImageNet set itself the extremely ambitious goal of "mapping the entire world of objects" (Gershgorn 2017), as explained by its co-creator, Stanford professor Fei-Fei Li. Just a few years later, through the collection and classification of millions of images gathered online, ImageNet had expanded to include over fourteen million labeled images, organized into more than twenty thousand categories, becoming one of the benchmark datasets for object recognition in the field of machine learning.

Today, just over fifteen years later, AI models for text-to-image, text-to-video, and machine vision, trained on billions of images and texts paired together, allow users to generate still and moving images from prompts written in natural language —i.e. human language—and to detect, recognize, and classify objects depicted in images, a mapping process achieved by systematically coupling images with words. However, the upshot of an artificial intelligence system trained on a dataset like ImageNet is that it can see only what it has learned to name; everything else remains in an undefined, nameless background.

Recent developments in AI technologies applied to images outline a new visual culture in which images and words are inseparable. AI introduces a series of systematic, algorithmic correlations that profoundly reorganize the relations between what can be seen and what can be said (Somaini 2024). It is a visual culture in which vision is tightly interwoven with language, where images are produced from words and texts, and in which the visible and the sayable are algorithmically interconnected. By contributing to the generation of these images, prompts act as a new kind of speech act, thus showing how language can be operative and become a form of action (Crawford & Paglen 2019).

Controlling the content of these datasets means controlling imagination and scope for visualization; it means holding mastery over the visible, over the boundary that separates what can be seen from what cannot. It also means being able to impose dominant styles and iconographies, making it difficult for users to escape them. The latent spaces where associations between prompts and outcomes take shape are in fact opaque and invisible to their users. Those who explore them are forced to proceed blindly, through trial and error, variation, adjustment, and unexpected discovery. What they find themselves faced with is an archive with a huge number of possible images, only some of which are actually visualized.

What all these digital databases have in common, however, is the fact that they propose the production of something new that is entirely grounded in the old. These tools rely on images of the past to generate representations of the present or future, with the concrete and growing risk—as has already been shown—of aligning with political visions that idealize a past that exists only in images

(Bogerts & Fielitz 2023; Meyer 2025), **creating structurally nostalgic visual worlds that reinforce political narratives based on stereotypes that are often hegemonial, imperialistic, racist, and sexist.** 1 In recent years, the works of artists such as Minne Atairu, Mushon Zer-Aviv, Kate Crawford, and Trevor Paglen, to name but a few, have highlighted and scrutinized the inconsistencies and biases inherent in the functioning of AI.

The rapid rise of AI over the past two years has made strikingly evident what in computer science is defined as the "semantic gap." This term describes the structural distance between things in the world and their linguistic or symbolic representation, i.e. the disconnect between the user's request and the outcome produced by the machine. Into this gap fall all those things that defy verbal description. This is far from secondary: while human language remains anchored to knowledge of the real world—we understand words because we have experience of them; we feel emotions and intentions linked to them, and we refer to a preexisting culture—the machine instead operates through automatisms and probability-based assumptions. Most of what we know we cannot explain; much of human thought exists outside linguistic consciousness, yet it constitutes a fundamental form of knowledge, one that takes shape through gestures, materials, lived space (Cotter 2019; Ingold 2013). Every translation into words entails a loss, an excess that goes unrecorded. Hence, the risk is for the complexity of what resists easy deciphering to be lost in the space that lies between words and images.

At a time when, day by day, AI is becoming an increasingly powerful and widespread tool to support our reading and shaping of the world, what then are the new responsibilities of artists, designers, and critics who work, design, and operate daily with images and words? In the contemporary era of visual hyperproduction and overinformation, images and words have been transformed into a continuous, fast, overabundant, and ever-accessible flow. It is therefore necessary to find strategies to contrast this perceptual overload, which often leads to a passive and superficial consumption of contents, hindering a critical and deeper understanding of reality. The saturation that defines our present risks confusing, numbing, and overwhelming its consumers, at a time when words and images no longer seem sufficient to explain the world. What, then, might be the role and value of artistic and creative practices in contextualizing and mediating these materials?

Between late 1974 and early 1975, American artist Martha Rosler was working in the heart of the Bowery—a New York neighborhood then known for its issues with drunkenness and urban decay—on a photographic series. The project, a photo-text installation consisting of twenty-four panels, features head-on views of storefronts and walls in the neighborhood, taken with a fixed lens from the edge of the street. No people are visible. Rosler's decision not to include human figures in her photographs but only traces of their passage constituted a counter-documentary practice, a rejection of the established conventions of documentary photography at the time. *The Bowery in two inadequate descriptive systems*, as the work is titled, focuses on the inevitable fallibility of text and words. The words do not describe the photographs, nor, conversely, do the photographs offer any illustrative explanation of the texts. By refusing to link text and image in a functional way, Rosler opens an unoccupied space of association between the two systems. As stated on the Whitney Museum of New York's website, the project interrogates "photographic conventions in ways that examine the authenticity associated with documentary photography and the unbalanced relationship between disenfranchised communities and their visual representations. […] The resulting disjunction—between words that refer to an all-too-human state and images devoid of people—suggests the inherent limitations of both photography and language as 'descriptive systems' to address a complex social problem." Through her practice, Rosler highlights the limits of representation: it is only in the attempt to place text and image in dialogue, in the negotiation between the two communicative systems, that a sense of reality may be produced—where it also becomes the viewer's task to join the dots.

In this sense, art and design take on a decisive role: they generate modes of knowledge that operate in the interstices of language and visuals, proposing alternative ways of perceiving, thinking, and feeling.

This tension is constitutive, insofar as the work does not attempt to state the real but to make it experienceable, rendering visible the discrepancy between the word, the image, and the world. From this perspective, the knowledge produced by art and design does not merely illustrate preexisting concepts, but creates embodied experiences that call into question the very idea of knowledge as mere representation. This critical stance becomes even more important today, at a time when information—which so often reaches us bereft of context—risks becoming mere background noise and propaganda.

Although in academia, and more generally within institutional systems of knowledge production, there persists a hierarchy that privileges the use of text, discursive logic, and numerical formalization over the forms of visual, material, and embodied knowledge proper to artistic and design practices, numerous scholars have highlighted how the continuity between making, thinking, and knowing are not simply supports for thought, but thought itself (Ingold 2013). The literature on artistic and design research has shown how these practices produce autonomous forms of knowledge, irreducible either to the sciences or to the humanities Donald Schön (1983), with his notion of "reflection-in-action," described the tacit knowledge that emerges from the work of creative professionals—a situated, dynamic knowledge not always translatable into propositional language. From similar observations, Nigel Cross spoke of "designerly ways of knowing" (2006), identifying cognitive modes specific to design, such as visual thinking, modeling, and iterative processes. These are forms of knowledge "distinct from the more usually recognized scientific and scholarly ways of knowing." While "scientists problem-solve by analysis, [...] designers problem-solve by synthesis. [...] They use 'codes' that translate abstract requirements into concrete objects. [...] Design offers opportunities for the development of a wide range of abilities in nonverbal thought and communication."

Despite a multitude of contributions over recent decades, embodied and material forms of knowledge still struggle to be acknowledged as fully legitimate. Research in art and design has long been judged according to parameters borrowed from the sciences rather than to criteria specific to creative practices (Frayling 1993). This epistemic imbalance is not without political consequences: the hierarchy that subordinates practice to language consolidates a logic of exclusion, resulting in unequal access to cultural and academic legitimacy. This imbalance is rooted in a long cultural and political history that has defined the parameters of what is recognized as legitimate knowledge. As Henk Borgdorff (2012) observes, the dominant consensus on what constitutes thought, knowledge, art, or culture is historically constructed and grounded in Enlightenment epistemology, which contributed to defining a paradigm centered on abstract rationality, empiricism, and measurement. But by doing so, it progressively marginalized many other forms of knowledge.

European colonial imposition exported and enforced this model as the prevailing one, relegating the material, embodied, and relational knowledge of over eighty percent of the world's population to the margins (Cotter 2019).

Acknowledging the validity of material and embodied knowledge does not mean denying the role of language but decentering it, restoring its function as complementary, as one of contextualization and mediation rather than as exclusive foundation. It means accepting that knowledge can manifest itself through materials, space, the body, and through relations and negotiations among these elements, and that such modes are not secondary or merely illustrative but constitutive. With its emphasis on the oral, material, and performative registers of knowledge, artistic research can be acknowledged as a privileged point of access to modes of understanding the world that exceed verbal language and which can become a valuable tool in helping us make sense of the complex and layered reality in which we are immersed.

Artistic research contributes to the pluralization of epistemology, beyond what may be exclusively linguistically formalized (Borgdorff 2012). By acknowledging that not everything can be translated into words, we open up spaces of legitimacy for forms of knowledge long excluded or marginalized. The value of these nonverbal knowledges is not only aesthetic but also political. It means recognizing that knowledge is always partial, as something

that goes beyond words, and that it is precisely in this excess that scope lies for new ways of exploring, understanding, and giving form to the world.

Barrett, Estelle and Barbara Bolt (eds.). *Practice as Research: Approaches to Creative Arts Enquiry.* London: I.B. Tauris, 2007.

Barrett, Estelle and Barbara Bolt (eds.). *Material Inventions: Applying Creative Arts Research.* London: I.B. Tauris, 2014.

Borgdorff, Henk. *The Conflict of the Faculties: Perspectives on Artistic Research and Academia.* Leiden: Leiden University Press, 2012.

Cotter, Lucy (ed.). *Reclaiming Artistic Research.* Amsterdam: Hatje Cantz / Amsterdam University of the Arts, 2019

Crawford, Kate and Trevor Paglen. "Excavating AI: The Politics of Training Sets for Machine Learning," September 10, 2019. https://excavating.ai.

Cross, Nigel. *Designerly Ways of Knowing.* London: Springer, 2006.

Frayling, Christopher. *Research in Art and Design.* London: Royal College of Art, 1993.

Gershgorn, Dave. "The Data That Transformed AI Research—and Possibly the World." *Quartz*, July 26, 2017. https://qz.com/1034972/the-data-that-changed-the-direction-of-ai-research-and-possibly-the-world/.

Ingold, Tim. *Making: Anthropology, Archaeology, Art and Architecture.* London: Routledge, 2013

Meyer, Roland. "KI-Bildgeneratoren sind Nostalgie–maschinen und Klischee–verstärker." *Woz.ch*, No. 20, May 15, 2025. https://www.woz.ch/2520/roland-meyer/ki-bild-generatoren-sind-nostalgie-maschinen-und-klischee-verstaerker.

Schön, Donald. *The Reflective Practitioner: How Professionals Think in Action.* New York: Basic Books, 1983.

Somaini, Andrea. "Le visible et l'énonçable. L'IA et les nouveaux liens algorithmiques entre images et mots." *Esthétiques artificielles* 2024/1: 47–58.

Whitney Museum of American Art. "*The Bowery in Two Inadequate Descriptive Systems.*" https://whitney.org/collection/works/8304.

Simone C Niquille

Obvious Questions Don't Exist: Uncertainty and Ambiguity as Knowledge Practices

Moving through space as a queer body, you stick out through difference. Coding appearance, presenting legibility, being mis/read through established patterns are all rituals familiar to the queer body. Computational ways of seeing introduce pattern recognition as a factual gaze verified by data. Under a computational gaze, difference becomes something to fix, uncertainty a problem to solve. Ambiguity and uncertainty are quickly rendered a threat in a statistical logic of perception. Yet I have come to value, rather than avoid, the friction of ambiguity as an existence and a practice—seeking spaces the system fails to fully capture or name.

My own queer experience of in/visibility and mis/reading has influenced my interest in face recognition technology and computational optics that "read" bodies at scale. The core of my practice is an investigation, documentation and resistance to how design and technology views bodies and knowledge as static units. In *Queer OS*, the scholar Kara Keeling describes "new media's eccentric temporalities and reliance on reading codes" and the potential of "queer as naming an orientation toward various and shifting aspects of existing reality," as a perpetually inquisitive and destabilizing force. In my practice, this operates as a critical investigation of computational optics and a refusal of its logic as certainty.

In my master thesis in 2013, I explored the value of the face in an age of computer vision and mass-circulated spam. Titled "FaceValue," it drew lines through the complexity of face recognition technology and its many applications: from Facebook's face-tagging feature, face.com's API applied by Google forum groups to identify individuals on CCTV footage following the 2012 London riots, to unsolicited website pop-ups and spam email inboxes populated with the portrait photos of unconsenting young women to lure clicks for profit. One of the works I created was a collection of t-shirts called Realface Glamouflage, a reference to the vegetation-imitating "Realtree" camouflage pattern developed for hunting. Instead of foliage, the t-shirts featured the faces of celebrity lookalikes. These faces were hard to tell apart from "the real version" for a human as well as a machine, with various degrees of success in simulation. The t-shirt was explicitly chosen as a simple enough article of clothing to circulate and be worn without question, while the pattern drew on the discomfort of being read, teasing the possibility of misrecognition through identity at the scale of a celebrity (lookalike). The intention of the t-shirts was not to hide the wearer. The pattern referenced dazzle camouflage: a technique developed in World War One to camouflage large objects such as naval vessels. Rather than making the object invisible, the aim of dazzle is to hide in plain sight by painting jagged patterns that make the object hard to read. 1 Behrens, Roy R., "Ship Shape, a Dazzle Camouflage Sourcebook" (2012). *Faculty Book Gallery.* 427. The Realface Glamouflage collection featured Barack Obama, Britney Spears, Michael Jackson, and Hillary Clinton. These subjects share a global level of popularity and distribution that rendered their faces universally recognizable. In the process of making the t-shirts, I had a WhatsApp conversation with Ilham Anas, 2 https://x.com/obamadoubleid a Barack Obama lookalike based in Indonesia whom I had met on Twitter. In a chat, he would describe the nuance of his work to me, explaining the care he took when selecting jobs "trying not to make the real Obama look bad."

Upon their release, the t-shirts struck a cord. This was the summer of 2013, and Edward Snowden had just leaked thousands of classified NSA documents revealing global surveillance programs. Computer vision, particularly face recognition, was exposed as a tool wielded by power for surveillance, policing, and control as much as it was also added as a convenience feature to electronic devices and interfaces. Public debate was quick to split between good and bad technologies. I don't find this binary opposition particularly useful as it ignores complexity and context (who, when, what, why) while transferring agency to the technology itself. Furthermore, it pushes a binary interpretation of the technology's functionality into right and wrong results, underlining the promise that appearance can be read successfully to reveal information, from emotions to gender, age, and motive. (Queer) bodies tend to defy the metrics by which these attributes are defined. Often enough, they reveal themselves to be subjective references and stereotypes masquerading behind computation. Researcher Adam Harvey has created an extensive body of work scrutinizing the underlying data and mechanisms of face recognition technology, as has the computer scientist Joy Buolamwini in her work with the Algorithmic Justice League and the artist and researcher Anna Ridler through the meticulous creation of her own image-training datasets, laying bare the decision-making and labor that machine-learning technology relies on.

The complexity of face recognition and computer vision at large is what drew me to it. Although cutting-edge, the technology draws on an age-old tangle of images, authorship, and agency, which are familiar queries in photography theory. Computational optics scaled these issues to the world at large and conjured up notions of world brains 3 In a series of talks and essays in 1937, H. G. Wells speculated on a "World Brain," as a world encyclopedia—a repository of scientifically established knowledge—that would spread enlightenment around the world and lead to global peace. Wells, known to readers today as the author of *The War of the Worlds* and other science-fiction classics, was imagining something akin to a predigital Wikipedia. The world encyclopedia would provide a summary of verified reality (in about forty volumes); it would be widely available, free of copyright, and draw on the latest technology. Of course, as Bruce Sterling points out in the foreword to this edition of Wells's work, the World Brain didn't happen; the internet did. And yet, Wells anticipated aspects of the internet, envisioning the World Brain as a technical system of networked knowledge (in Sterling's words, a "hypothetical super-gadget"). Wells's optimism about the power of information might strike readers today as naïvely utopian, but possibly also inspirational. (description from MIT Press.) **and eyes of providence.**

While data to train these mythical machines is limited, there is such an overwhelming amount of it that it is falsely thought to be all-encompassing. The questions at the core remains the same: Who is capturing whom for what reason? Who has the right to an image?

The Realface Glamouflage t-shirts got picked up by the media. However, they were stripped of the narrative and ironically taken at face value. Rather than a pattern of celebrity lookalikes that could fool humans and machines alike, the t-shirts were reported as anti-surveillance devices. The nuance of the discussion was lost and the design turned into a passive solution: wear the t-shirt → confuse computer vision → continue life. Rather than systemic change or fundamental discussions about computer vision, its role as surveillance technology or societies obsession with reading and classifying bodies, the t-shirts fit neatly into an antiquated definition of design as a solutionist discipline, in line with mainstream desires to erase ambiguity, newly inspired by the certainty machine-learning mimicks. In the press, the entangled relationship between recognition, identity politics, and image rights that I wanted the t-shirts to embody was flattened. There is never a wrong moment to invoke Laurie Anderson, and this quote from her meditation teacher sums it up nicely: "If you think technology will solve your problems, you don't understand technology—and you don't understand your problems." 4 https://www.wired.com/beyond-the-beyond/2020/03/

laurie-anderson-machine-learning-artist-residence/ **A t-shirt won't save you. I created the t-shirts not as a form of salvation but as props of our current reality, a filmset we are capturing in real time with cameras pointing and mounted everywhere.**

Realface Glamouflage's portrayal in the press taught me two lessons that informed my practice from then on: (1) my work is not a bug report and (2) asking questions is sufficient labor. What is lost when we flatten differences into technical problems to be solved?

I – THE BUG REPORT

In 1947, computer scientist and mathematician Grace Hopper was operating the Mark II computer at Harvard University when it suddenly malfunctioned. The root of the issue turned out to be a moth stuck to a relay. The incident is widely cited as the origin story of the "bug report," a document that describes a software error to its developers. The way in which Realface Glamouflage was interpreted as a "fix" to a problem made me see the project as a bug report. The t-shirts pointed out a system's flaws (face recognition wasn't able to tell apart a printed face from a real one, or a lookalike from a celebrity). Inadvertently, Realface Glamouflage could contribute to the improvement of face recognition. Not quite the type of design research I had in mind. Once released to a public, the project took on a life, and narrative, of its own. An important lesson I took with me was

that there is only a certain amount of control you can have over how a work is read, twisted, turned, and framed in the public eye. Likewise, the *Wired* journalist who wrote the first article on the project misgendered me by using male pronouns, wrongly assuming that a tech-adjacent project had to be authored by a guy. Even without a visible body, purely based on the project through an email conversation, mis/reading of identity and authorship is possible, revealing the stereotypes of the tech industry.

The bug report stuck with me as a research method. An exercise I do with students is to write a thank-you letter. 5 For an archive of past thank you letters: https://pt.ma-id.cloud/index.php?title=Thank_You Instead of reporting a problem, this text expresses gratitude for a piece of software, a sliver of code, a specific feature or an interface update that one is appreciative of. It shifts the perspective ever so slightly from associating critical thinking with seeking what is wrong to identifying what is delightful. Furthermore, it requires the letter writer to identify a recipient: who is responsible for the thing I am writing about? In 2025, it feels like a cliché to point out the nameless convention of software development. The "black box" metaphor referring to the opaque inner workings of a software, an algorithm or the system that created it points to the invisible labor and erratic politics often associated with the industry. While open source culture presents an antidote and thrives on documentation and community (while certainly not with its troubles), identifying who is behind the Adobe

Photoshop batch processing feature is a bit harder. The thank you letter thus becomes a software history crawl. This information is not readily indexed by a search engine, but it might surface somewhere in the depths of an old forum post, a low-resolution YouTube video, or an interview in *Byte* magazine accessed via the Internet Archive. Its value is in understanding how the digital tools we use and depend on have come to be what they are. This is crucial to understanding where we might want to head next, and how to get there. The digital tools we use to create our imaginaries are coded using someone's worldview. Names are not only authorship; they are also access to understanding an operation. Alternative methods of knowledge-making practices, such as the parametric truth lab or writing a thank you letter, create space for those who are habitually rendered illegible in dominant and formal knowledge systems.

II – A MILLION QUESTIONS

> The limits of my language mean the limits of my world.
> The limits of my categories mean the limits of my world.
> The limits of my data mean the limits of my world.
> And I am left with a million questions.
> Language Fails Me.

The first-person narrator of my film *HOMESCHOOL* (2019) sounds equally puzzled and frustrated while paraphrasing Ludwig Wittgenstein's writing on language and the limits of thought from the *Tractatus Logico-Philosophicus*, reinterpreted for the age of computer vision. Are the limits of knowledge tied to language, just as machine learning's capacity depends on the limits of training data? In *HOME-SCHOOL*, the training data for domestic computer vision is the main character, rendering fully visible the otherwise invisible. Although, as the viewer discovers over the course of the film, the data's visibility does not guarantee legibility. A chair is mistaken for a baby stroller: aren't they both for sitting? The struggle of legibility and mis/reading is all too recognizably queer. In the film, the narrator takes the viewer on a tour of a strange interior: objects are oddly arranged, traces of a logicless plot, eerie familiarity clashing with the unknown. Each frame has a varying degree of grain, pixels pushing up against each other, resulting in a smeared resolution. The image and the voice are thus equally full of query.

The narrator recounts anecdotes I've been told by the computer scientists creating computer vision for automated vacuum cleaners, to assist in their navigation of a home. Speaking directly to the individuals involved in building these tools is crucial to my practice. Through conversation, I learn what I couldn't from reading research papers or press clips: the failed experiments, surprise discoveries, dreams, and imaginaries. Like the thank you letter, the conversation is a gateway into informal knowledge. These conversations contextualize the technology to a small degree, offering a glimpse into the assumptions and decisions are taken during its development. Being in conversation has become a practice of pursuing ambiguity. I don't seek answers but rather attempt to uncover the uncertainties and doubts that linger on the fringes of these technologies. As Matthew Fuller and Eyal Weizman describe their approach to the "introspection" of digital tools in Investigative Aesthetics: "It is through critical use, and in practice, that contradictions, biases and limitations can be most fully identified, understood and, when possible, exposed." 6 M. Fuller & E. Weizman (2021). *Investigative Aesthetics: Conflicts and Commons in the Politics of Truth*. Verso, p. 16. A major part of my practice is to use the technologies I am researching to create the work itself, 7 In the case of *HOMESCHOOL*, the film was created with the 3D models of SceneNet-RGBD: a dataset for indoor computer vision training created by Imperial College London (2016). The visuals used an array of workflows and processes critical to creating a computer-generated image or, on the contrary, to train a computer-vision model, but are not meant as an "end product" for human consumption. These include depth maps, AI image denoisers, and ambient occlusion maps. yet interviews and conversations are what makes the work come alive. They hold knowledge that escapes formal systems and offer moments to share doubt.

Asking a question will never not feel vulnerable. Is it exposing incompetence? Does a lack of knowledge strip me of my right to be in the room? Getting to ask a question requires access first. Access to a room, a person, an email, a Zoom call. I've worn plenty of hats to try and initiate a conversation: that of researcher, student, writer, educator, CGI animator, visual culture researcher, software historian, and critical data studies fellow. The list goes on like the various profile pictures people have for their different social media personas. My aim when entering into interdisciplinary conversations is to be able to speak across language: we might be saying the same thing but in a different room with different words.

A million questions demand inclusion in conversation, to remain unsure and to embrace the quest, not the destination. The beauty is that, over time, many things turn out to be conversation threads with their own stories to tell: be it a dataset, a software interface, an image, or a GitHub repository.

SOFTWARE AS MATERIAL

In her essay "On Software, or the Persistence of Visual Knowledge," Wendy Hui Kyong Chun points to "software's new status as common sense." At the Master Information Design department of the Design Academy Eindhoven, I established the parametric truth lab. Its name derives from a term coined in 2016 to describe my practice. Setting out from the work around FaceValue and Reface Glamouflage, I investigated the technologies used to translate bodies into numbers. This work tied together the development of 3D scanning, ergonomic design software and forensic policing strategies from the nineteenth century. What they had in common was the will to index the human shape for means of identification, legibility, and control. **Parametric truth is the creation and justification of new realities through software.** 8 Simone C Niquille "Parametric Truth," in K. Maurer, R. Munck Petersen, D. Routhier, K. Veel, & K. Wellendorf (eds.). *Aesthetics of Machine Vision: Critical terms and Ideas* (forthcoming, 2025–26). MIT Press. **When software is a dependency to the extent that it is deemed as common sense, knowledge that all humans are expected to know, telling it apart from reality becomes as difficult as the lookalike from the celebrity.**

The lab is a space to question the obvious: here questions are only "sufficient labor" as pointed out earlier, but the desired practice, until the default melts away and its construction shows. It offers time and resources to tinker mentally and practically. Darren Wershler, Lori Emerson, and Jussi Parikka describe the lab as "a hybrid knowledge environment." 9 D. Wershler, L. Emerson & J. Parikka. *The Lab Book: Situated Practices in Media Studies.* Minneapolis: University of Minnesota Press, 2022. **In the case of the parametric truth lab, this means creating a space to talk about and research software without the need for "technical know-how." The atmosphere of the lab is akin to the computational culture Winnie Soon and Geoff Cox describe as a "means to engage with programming to question existing technological paradigms and further create changes in the technical system."** 10 W. Soon & G. Cox (2020). *Aesthetic Programming: A Handbook of Software Studies.* Open Humanities Press. **You don't need to know** how to code to join the lab. Before perhaps creating a change to the technical system itself, the lab offers space first and foremost to question technological paradigms, and sit with them. In education, the emphasis is all too often on software as productivity tool, carrying your project towards completion or evoking a particular aesthetic. I've received invitations over the years to teach "how-to" workshops. I've always struggled with the request—it made me feel like an imposter. Everyone works differently with their own thinking process. The best software supports individual workflows rather than dictating a "right way." Learning a software is not about being taught but about exploring its capabilities and wiring your own language and aesthetic through it. Instead of tutorials, the parametric truth lab proposes ways to critically engage with software beyond productivity. Rather than making as producing, we might spend a day exploring a software we have always been curious about but never had the time to use. Of course we cannot ignore the multitude of factors that make one opt for a software for a project, from the office one works at to file compatibility issues, to operating systems and the time it takes to learn a new program. Yet if we only look at our hindrances, a new world will never be made.

It takes a lot of unlearning—and perhaps also a dose of sincerity, which should not be mistaken for naiveté—to question the things we take for granted. Jack Halberstam speaks of "little thoughts shared widely […] hunches, whims, fancies," 11 J. Halberstam

(2011). *The queer art of failure*, Duke University Press. **Inviting intuition over rationality, the parametric truth lab is a space of uncertainty, of un/learning, and of the seemingly insignificant. While software presents an attitude of expertise, I believe no question is too basic to direct at it. What one person calls basic may be fundamental to someone else.**

Matteo Antoniazzi
ABCDEMINDED

In June 1973, British musician Robert Wyatt, intoxicated during a party in London, fell from the bathroom window of a fourth-floor flat. The injury shattered his spine, and rendered him paraplegic. On his hospital bed, he continued to compose, building on the experimental ethos of his previous legendary ensemble Matching Mole, what would become his second solo album. The following July saw the release of *Rock Bottom*, an elegiac record comprised of songs drifting between dream and waking life in a continuous flow of oceanic currents, interminglings of rock and jazz sensibilities perpetually oscillating between the English pastoralism of Canterbury and the Venetian isolation of La Giudecca. Tracks four and five are dedicated to his partner Alfreda Benge, the Austrian poet and artist whose name emerges, echoed and fragmented, in the lyrics' puzzling textures:

> Not nit not nit no not
> nit folly bololey
> Alifi my larder
> Alifi my larder
> I can't forsake you or
> Forsqueak you
> Alifi my larder
> Alifi my larder

1   R. Wyatt, (1974). "Alife" from *Rock Bottom*

Cast in a register of despair, what takes shape is an intimate language shared by two people, a language of lovers that Wyatt employs during his hospital stay with his partner by his side, tending to him. From this intimate code arises a lyrical portrayal of his wife, at once heartfelt and unromantic, tender and crude. Wyatt's language is shaped by Benge's poetic sensibility; indeed, she would soon become co-author of much of his lyrical output in a practical act of shared authorship, in which a lexicon is forged of which the meaning is hermetically and jealously guarded, yet whose emotional resonance remains readily accessible.

This blend of English with the couple's private parlance recalls other Anglophone experiments in lexical and syntactic hybridity—above all, T.S. Eliot's *The Waste Land*, also written during a period of hospitalization, and James Joyce's monumental dream-poem fifteen years in the making *Finnegans Wake*. Joyce's text features the neologism that lends its name to this brief reflection: "abcdeminded," 2 J. Joyce, (1939). *Finnegans Wake.* a wordplay also dear to **Marshall McLuhan** 3 McLuhan, M. (1970). *Culture is Our Business.* used to describe Joyce's literati contemporaries: "absent-minded" setting out from the rigid and conditioning formal structures exemplified by the alphabetic control of language, a figure of the mind's internal dispositions yielding to the pressures of the external world. And yet Joyce, paradoxically, employs the very tools of these *abcdeminded* for his literary delirium; but the language of the Wake, much like the language of Wyatt's falls, *is not quite it*: Joyce weaponizes this linguistic conditioning by turning the alphabet's constraint into the grounds for his linguistic aberration. The Wake's language is not simply broken; it is methodically disassembled and repurposed, becoming a deviation from linguistic normativity, and reclaiming language as a projective medium rather than a vessel of clear communication, highlighting the inherent polyglossia of any language, understood here as a medium, whether composed of words, moving images, gestures, sounds, or hybrid assemblage of various materials.

It seems only natural then that Bolzano, of all cities, should be the one to pose so pointed a question as that at the heart of this publication: what happens when words fail? What occurs when, in a historically mercantile urban agglomerate where three languages are spoken 4 Südtiroler Informatik AG | Informatica Alto Adige SPA, News & pubblicazioni | Istituto provinciale di statistica | Provincia autonoma di Bolzano – Alto Adige, on Istituto provinciale di statistica and a plurality of nationalities intersect and coexist, 5 Demographic balance of foreign population and foreign resident population by gender, as found on demo.istat.it. we come face to face with the inadequacy of the verbal tools at hand, and find ourselves in a moment of astonished acknowledgement, communicating without needing to obey the rules that communication, understood here in all its most cumbersome connotations, imposes through its intrinsic representational inefficiency? One is forced to point, to stammer, to gesture in both oddly persuasive and awkward ways; words whose very failure becomes their might are invented; language is distorted and torn, stitched and glued together from scraps and fragments of mutually alien tongues in a lexical juggling act that simultaneously sublimates the opacity of incommunicability and the desperate desire to be understood. From this, amid the hands and the tip of the tongue, we discover a mongrel, unstable language of necessity: a polysemic pidgin, drifting and rootless, a fleeting and circumstantial babble born of error. This is an intimate, articulatory distortion of language taking place within an unbridgeable gap: instant dialects conjured by distance, exclusive and singular to nearby interlocutors, just like Wyatt's "language of lovers," or the "lingua a due" that Andrea Zanzotto explored at such length. It is precisely *petèl*, that affectionate, untranslatable nonsense with its "liquid sonorities and gurgling accumulation" [sonorità liquida e l'affastellarsi gorgogliante], 6 Zanzotto, A. (1976). *Filò per il Casanova di Fellini, con una lettera e cinque disegni di F. Fellini*, Venice, Edizioni del Ruzante. murmured between parents and children and given great attention by the poet from Treviso, 7 Among others, "Elegia in petèl," "Nota al Filò," "Pasqua di maggio," "Profezie o memorie o giornali murali" by the same author. and that stands as a viable hypothesis for such a language of necessity. It is transient, as it exists on the threshold between pure sound and the signifying word; ambiguous, and therefore expansive in interpretive potential; necessary, insofar as it offers the most immediate means of mutual understanding: not to comprehend meaning, but to *create* it.

It thus offers a sidestep away from official language, a tangent composed of words outside the dictionary but already, and undeniably, *language*, even before being corrected by linguistic norm, a *mischmasch* of allogenic material, an activator of a transference of meanings and signifiers that transpose the need for coexistence into a mellifluous dialect. *Petèl*, after all, is known by everyone but spoken by no one.

In editing the bilingual poetry series *Ardilut*, in the light of his reading of twentieth-century Italian poetic production, Giorgio Agamben also introduces the ever-present and characteristic diglossia of Italian linguistic artisans: a condition in which, alongside the official language—that of education, politics, law, communication, but also of unity—one always carries one's dialect. That is, the language of the family, of the workplace, of village festivities and domestic life, of fragmentation, folklore, and tribal mythology. Let us be clear, though: it is by no means my intention to turn this text into a nostalgic homage to a certain idea of "popular culture" or other culinary staples: the roots of that culture have long since been severed and dried out, roots which—the above-mentioned culture being an oral one—now survive only in the tools once adopted for education, of which the ossified remains are now exhibited in some "Museum of Peasant Culture and Civilization." In keeping with Agamben's reading, 8 https://www.doppiozero.com/il-bilinguismo-della-poesia what I mean here by "bilingualism"—a phenomenon which, in Bolzano, splinters even further—is the deep-seated tension running through every true linguistic expression, it is the fertile conflict from which all poetry is born: a fumbling with language in its entirety, not only with words, but with the material issue that emerges each time we set out to make some *thing*.

Working on language means working on a shared hypothesis of how the world is read, on the definition of that imaginative horizon towards which one moves. And in engaging with this practice hands on, one ends up unmooring material alphabets, salvaging many tools, modes, materials, and technologies from the mire of function into which they had sunk. This is an undisciplined and liquid maneuver, composing fleeting and hybrid, insufficient and mumbling, new momentary dialects complete with their slips, aphasias, stammerings, and forgettings.

To disarticulate a language is to use it without claiming ownership, to renounce the market value of immediacy and the demand for instant comprehension. It means dwelling in that unresolvable gap between the urge to speak and the ability to do so; imposing a certain difficulty, generating estrangement, opening up discursive and conflictual spaces, and thereby allowing for stratifications of meaning.

Each authorial or artisanal action marks a difference that translates into political evidence. This, ultimately, is the *consequentially political* act of knowledge production through practical gestures: alternatives are proposed, efficiency and function are set aside, and within the ambiguity intrinsic to this protean glossolalia, new, turbulent, and provocative possibilities emerge. Yet within this act, there need not be any consolatory or salvific mission, no drive to improve our condition. Instead, it is a matter of overwhelming, of disengaging from this redemptive duty, of breaking down and remixing the alphabets mentioned earlier, centrifuging, unpacking, and kneading anew the elements of the totalizing symbolic order. 9 In this regard, I recommend reading Leo Bersani's extraordinary book, *The Culture of Redemption.* For example, one need only consider the body of experimental cinematic work that emerged in the mid-1960s and flourished over the following decade. These works, often composed using multiple film stocks, frame-by-frame interventions, celluloid scratching, temporal loops, overlays, and negative exposures, did not merely probe the aesthetic and formal possibilities of the moving image; they systematically dismantled the illusion of cinematic transparency. Artists such as Tony Conrad, Hollis Frampton, and Michael Snow constructed films that foregrounded the mechanical operations of projection and perception itself. Frampton's *Zorn's Lemma*, for instance, replaces narrative with alphabetical sequence, exhausting the symbolic potential of letters until meaning dissolves into perceptual rhythm. Meanwhile, Conrad's *The Flicker* reduces moving images to their physiological minimum, confronting the viewer with retinal shock rather than aesthetic pleasure. These works succeeded in reframing the cinematic apparatus as a site of pitiful failure: through methodical collapse, there comes the revelation of the inefficiency of representation itself. Much like the poetic and linguistic works discussed earlier, structural cinema presented us with a field where form has to fail in order to find new ground, where rupture is the only honest grammar left to recontextualize all that surrounds it.

Looking further back, we can see how linear perspective too, once codified as the "legitimate" mode of representation, figuration, and modeling of reality, like any model or approximation of complexity, inevitably carried with it a discrepancy between the technically produced image and the retinal one. Thus, the distortions and forced alignments inherent in its method were inscribed even in the raw data that fed the modelling process itself. 10 Panofsky, E. (1927). *Perspective as symbolic form.* From there arise the distortions and deformations, the disaggregations and fragmentations, the dislocations, torsions, and aberrations, all multiplying diversely across reality: deviations that may remain minimal, or that may grow until something imperceptibly shifts. Provisional grammars that falter, models that betray the world they seek to model. One must remain in the background, out of focus, working instead on what frames the whole. To recontextualize, to recontextualize ourselves; to inhabit the background noise, to distort the foundational data—language itself—and to witness the ensuing avalanche. Hosted beneath a sheltering tongue, within this collective assemblage, we become parasites of form, conceptual agents of mutualism and symbiosis who, through mischief and playful transgression, overturn the entire arrangement of the dwelling we temporarily inhabit. Only to dismantle it again, reframing it askew in search of new openings, formulas for beginning anew: shaping material dialects of absence, ever caught in a motion of falling, wavering until they collapse, shattering into a dust that settles on all things. Gradually, breath by breath, we are infiltrated by these new and elegantly failed material somersaults, disconcerting postures, and unexpectedly frustrating forms of mobility. These dialects deterritorialize the "major language," 11 Deleuze, G., & Guattari, F. (2004). EPZ *Thousand Plateaus*. A&C Black. placing it in a state of continuous variation, a stammering of itself. Becoming estranged from one's own language means setting it in motion into a continuous, ever-shifting, and revitalizing failure.

Samuel Beckett, who also made the formal failure of his mother tongue his dialect, said it best: "To be an artist is to fail, as no one else dares to fail, that failure is his world and withdrawal from it desertion, art, and craft, good stewardship." 12 Beckett, S. (1965). *Proust and Three Dialogues with Georges Duthuit*. Calder and Boyars. For no language, no manner, will ever be capable of saying everything. The distillation of attitudes into material forms will never be a process free of interference, missteps, or slips. It will often require footnotes and rewritings, but I believe that creating means doing so dangerously, pushing the choices we make to their extreme consequences, and rejecting the notion of working downward toward

safe compromises. And this act entails exposing oneself, necessarily, to its very opposite. For in some way,
every intrusion always corresponds to an extrusion,
and from every stumble, from every small and intimate discomfort, there follow others, subsequent
and multiple, in their renewed internal differences.

Francesca Verga

Thinking Through Gesture: Choreographic Writing and Writing Choreography

During the 1960s and '70s—across New York, the West Coast, and Europe—a heterogeneous array of artistic practices radically challenged the formal and disciplinary conventions of making art. This was a moment of epistemic fracture, a paradigmatic reconfiguration in which dance abandoned traditional scenic architectures; choreography unfolded in the moment of the construction of its gestures, writing in dematerialized improvisation or disintegrated into nonlinear flows; and performance asserted itself as a transversal language capable of traversing gesture, word, image, and space. In this context of widespread experimentation, many artists began to question not so much what art expresses as *what it does*, and more precisely how thought can emerge *in practice*, rather than preceding it. Thought no longer precedes action as a schema or plan, but manifests as an embodied process, activated through gesture, body, and the concrete temporality of doing. This process traverses both performance as such, and inextricably the very act of writing, which as we might recall can, has been, and perhaps sometimes must—with its structure and language—be constructed in the very moment of thought, or imagined in the very moment of gesture. As if we were able to formulate the thought at the exact moment of speech, the writing at the moment of the hand gesture; seeking perfection in the very act of acting.

At a time when dominant models of representation and knowledge were being called into question (in relation to various strands of feminism), many female artists in those years began to interrogate language's form and structure, opposing narrative and logical linearity as normative devices. Fragmented gesture, a present body, and discontinuous speech thus became tools for thinking differently, outside an ordered and hierarchical construction of meaning. The performative and visual practices of artists like Martha Rosler, Adrian Piper, Carolee Schneemann, Ana Mendieta, Valie Export, and many others belong to this genealogy, where female subjectivity does not present itself as identity but as process, tension, and fracture. This process also involved obsessive and reflexive writing projects in which authors did not merely transcribe a narrative flow, but constantly confronted the process of thought and language as they appeared on the page. This creative gesture was asserted as an act of simultaneous fabrication of meaning—a praxis in which writing is freed from the mere transport of predefined content only to become a field of dynamic experimentation, an agora of inner dialogue and dialectical tension between immediate intuition and metatextual reflection. It is a self-analytical exercise that is not limited to representation but continually interrogates itself, embracing uncertainty and fragmentariness not as limits but as methodological tools to probe unexplored horizons of meaning. In such a context, writing also freed itself from formal constraints, rejecting rigid structures to become a fluid and mutable expression of thought.

In the gap between reality and language, post-modern choreography practices are inserted, or at least the use of movement as an ontologically autonomous language, where the body is no longer a mere vehicle for a prepackaged message, but stands as an archive of gestures irreducible to words. In this corporeal device, gestural materiality unfolds, eluding conventional semantic categories, translating into a lexicon of fragments, residues, and nodes; revealing another subterranean, resistant dimension of experience that challenges the primacy of discourse and stands as a zone of indeterminacy and resistance to established meaning.

In the works of Trisha Brown, Yvonne Rainer, and Simone Forti, the body becomes a bearer of knowledge—a space in which one learns. Their practices, arising amid dance, the visual arts, and performance in 1960s New York—especially around the key experimental choreographic and interdisciplinary hub of the Judson Dance Theater—shifted reflection on knowledge into movement. Choreographic writing does not illustrate concepts, nor does it tell stories: it practices presence, inhabiting time and space. In Trisha Brown's *Accumulation* (1971), a minimal gesture repeats and expands—not to signify, but to exist as process. The piece was built on a simple structure: each new gesture adds to the preceding one, creating a chain of movements that slowly expands over time. The title itself, *Accumulation*, is not a metaphorical but a compositional device: every action in the performance (raising an arm, turning the head, bending the torso) is stripped of narrative or expressive intentionality. The movement reveals itself in its pure temporal existence, as if selfconstructing in the moment. This performative mode embodies another idea of subjectivity: that of a conscious, present body that thinks by doing, enacting a learning process that seems innate, reforming the gesture, not "at the service" of content to convey but as content in its own right, in its exactness and opaque legibility. Artist and choreographer Yvonne Rainer similarly refused spectacle—primarily through her *No Manifesto* (1965) and works like *Trio A* (1966)—thinking through action, relying on the body (its weight, hesitation, and gravity) as a form of knowing that cannot be translated into verbal language. The body acts without explanation or interpretation, becoming a Fluxus manifesto. Rainer works with everyday gestures, minimal expenditure of energy, repetition, and error—all elements that transform the body into a living archive.

In both artists, dance becomes embodied writing: nontextual, opposing language's clarity with productive ambiguity that cannot be fully codified or rendered in words. This tension between doing and thinking simultaneously pervaded many American postmodern dance practices: Simone Forti also worked on improvised "constructions" that required performers to decide in real time; and Joan Jonas —choreographer and performer on New York's postmodern scene—developed visual and performative research in which the human figure, movement, space, and image become cognitive tools. In Jonas' *Mirror Pieces* (1969–1971), for example, the body reflects and refracts through mirroring surfaces, building a choreography of instability and perception. It is not about illustrating meaning: the gesture is thought, happening as it is performed—it forms through movement, inevitably present.

Each of these choreographies is of course also a form of nonlinear, nonalphabetic but deeply structured writing. In this sense, the body in artistic and choreographic practice becomes a technology of knowledge alternative to the word: errant, intimate, and profoundly alive.

At the same time, a similar shift occurred in writing, where a number of writers began to dismantle the idea of text as a closed object and writing as the transcription of a preformed thought. In their practice, writing became a corporeal, uncertain, exploratory action—a form of thinking carried out while writing. By abandoning linearity, women found the chance to escape a language that had constructed them as objects—breaking the canon and exiting structure. Examples range from visual poetry groups (including the Gruppo 70 in Italy) to literary experimentation, to writers engaging with the word in radically experimental ways.

Remaining in the same period and geographic area but moving from choreography to writing understood as an almost performative gesture—imbued with desire, materiality, and the unknown—Kathy Acker (though quite trans-local since the 1980s) and Bernadette Mayer developed writing practices that were deeply corporeal, open, and contaminated. Acker rewrites, cuts, and pastes pornographic, philosophical, and autobiographical texts—turning writing into a punk, subversive gesture that breaks with all linearity (expanding on Burroughs's cut-up technique). Consider *Politics* (1972), one of her earliest selfpublished texts, which circulated in underground and feminist circles—an unstructured work fractured between sexual, theoretical, and dreamlike languages—or the literary cutups of *The Childlike Life of the Black Tarantula by the Black Tarantula* (1973–75). Mayer, on the other hand, explored writing accompanying life in real time, perhaps more intimate but equally radical, such as in her *Memory* project (1971), documenting every day of a month with words and photographs, or *Midwinter Day* (1982), written in a single day: December 22, 1978, the shortest day of the year.

In this sense, writing approaches dance, performance, and gesture. Just as in Trisha Brown's work movement is accumulated, decomposed, and discovered while happening, so in these writers' texts does writing present itself as a perceptive, uninterrupted flow, almost pregrammatical. Yet one of the most extreme examples of the 1970s that comes to mind is that of a Brazilian naturalized Ukrainian writer: *Água Viva* (1973) by Clarice Lispector. Perhaps a book that does not tell but that happens, in the absolute present of feeling. We might even say *Água Viva* is not merely a text but behaves like a body in action—a verbal organism that breathes, vibrates, stumbles, and expands, like a choreographic score. Lispector does not write about something but writes while something happens—and that something is consciousness itself shaping in the word, even prior to syntax.

These artistic, choreographic, and literary practices do not merely share poetics, but they propose an epistemology of the body and gesture, in which knowing is not possession but traversing, experiencing, and remaining in process. Both choreographers and writers in the 1970s pursued an art that does not represent but which acts. Art that rejects the separation between subject and object, thought and gesture, idea and matter. Whether in the moving body or the writing hand, thought emerges through *doing* —and for this very reason remains alive, open, irreducible to any single form.

Today, these concerns have been absorbed both into artistic practices involving movement and into writing, curating—inevitably—and those professional contexts in which the practice itself becomes a form of thought: where doing and thinking are not separate, but unfold simultaneously. What emerges now is an idea of art conceived more as process than product. On the post-postmodern horizon, many artistic and performative practices seem to relinquish ironic distance and the primacy of concept, restoring to practice an epistemic role: *thought* no longer precedes the work, but is constructed within the gesture itself, in the materiality of doing, in the immediacy of the acting body—again, *hic et nunc*.

In a present marked by systemic crises—ecological, political, and epistemological—and by a pervasive sense of instability and insatiability, the experimental practices of women artists and choreographers from the 1970s prove remarkably relevant, not as models to be replicated, but as devices to be critically reactivated. They continue to offer tools for thinking about art, the body, subjectivity, and collectivity in non-normative ways. Their work invites us to consider a form of situated knowledge, one that arises from the body, in the immediacy of the gesture, and in relation to context. To inhabit uncertainty today—just as then—does not mean abandoning form, but building it through movement, tension, and in the temporality of action. In this sense, contemporary practices that foreground process, failure, vulnerability, and dialogue between languages seem to receive and transform that legacy, driving it toward new configurations. This is not imitation but situated translation: perhaps a way of taking a stance within one's own time through reflective doing, which holds together experience, affect, and critical thought. Whether in performance or in writing, what remains is perhaps the urgency of embodied knowledge (one that cannot be separated from life) and of a practice that continually questions its own role and its conditions of existence.

Today, dance has come ever closer to life, to the ordinary gesture, to improvisation as a practice of listening, and to performance as an open and collective process. Rooted in this genealogy is a mode of creating dance that does not seek form as a fixed object but as relation. Movement is no longer subordinate to a predetermined choreographic design, but emerges as the outcome of situated listening —attention to the environment, to gravity, to the other. In this light, choreography no longer comes across as a closed composition but as an epistemological practice, an open and relational medium.

Many contemporary choreographic and writing practices seem to extend this legacy—characteristic of the 1970s—inscribing it within today's discursive and political urgencies. In Italy, there is a proliferation of practices that inhabit uncertainty as method, construction essentially as a gesture of the present. Consider, for instance, the work of Claudia Castellucci, who often explores gesture as a radically autonomous language; or the subtle, attentive writing of Ginevra Lamberti; or the multiple selves of Claudia Durastanti. Though diverse, these experiences share with the practices of the 1970s the conviction that gesture is not meant to illustrate thought, but is itself thought: alive, fragile, impulsive, and situated.

The work of Annamaria Ajmone is fully situated within this perspective. Her practice is grounded in an idea of the body as threshold, as a permeable organism in continuous metamorphosis. Ajmone creates performative environments in which the body does not display itself but undergoes a phase of mutation; it does not represent, but is traversed by temporal flows, ecological tensions, and affective sedimentations. Works such as *I pianti e i lamenti dei pesci fossili* (2024), *NO RAMA* (2019), and *To Be Banned from Rome* (2017) trigger perceptual devices that suspend linear time, destabilize the coordinates of stage identity, and also engage with improvisation. In this context, the body becomes a zone of passage, an unstable interface.

A kindred approach—though rooted in different cultural and geographical coordinates—may be found in the research of finnish choreographer Anna Maria Häkkinen. Her practice interrogates submerged genealogies of dance, activating the body as an affective archive, as a site of rewriting and re-inscription. In works such as *Afterglow, Low Lingering Slips of Light* (2025), Häkkinen brings forth a dance that is at once critical gesture and a practice of desire, drawing on minimalist dance while exploring release, surrender, time, autonomy, and cooperation. In this piece, Häkkinen revisits the figure of Lucinda Childs—a central voice in the Judson Dance Theater—thus paying homage to that era, through a work that combines the harp and electronic music.

In both Ajmone and Häkkinen, as well as in other contemporary choreographic practices, we witness a specific articulation of choreography as a practice of relation and decentering: a decentering of the subject–author, of movement as fixed meaning.

Choreography thus unfolds through relation. These artistic practices do not offer definitive answers, but open up spaces of possibility. They share a common sense of urgency: not to represent a subject, but to create space for a vulnerable, situated, and unstable coexistence. In a time marked by crisis and precarity, they reject linearity, subject autonomy, and formal closure, only to affirm a form of knowledge that is relational and embodied. Writing and dancing thus become acts of resistance and care, gestures through which to inhabit the present critically. It is in this entanglement of body and language, of vulnerability and processuality, that I believe a radical politics of gesture takes shape—not as a method for representing reality, but as its continual reinvention.

Silvio Lorusso
No Problem:
Design School
as Promise

GRAPHIC DESIGN IS SHIT
CODING IS SHIT
ALL I WANT IS REVENGE
—Sticker found in Berlin

THE PROMISE

A promise is something that is actively put forward. It involves intent and expectation. It is a performative speech act: an utterance that, hopefully, lives up to what it says. A promise is fulfilled when an intended future, that is now in the past, finally aligns with the present. That is when the speech act meets its so-called condition of felicity.

What kind of promise does design education involve? Does it relate to the present of education or to the future of work? What are the forces that shape it? How is it fulfilled and by whom? Who has the authority to sanction its fulfillment? Let us consider educational promises in general. first of all, they are not unilateral but reciprocal. It is not just the *promisor*, namely the school organization, in cooperation with or in opposition to the market and society, that is supposed to fulfill it ("We'll give you knowledge, skills and a space to develop them"), but the individual *promisee* as well, the student, as they guarantee effort and participation ("I'll make it worthwhile").

Things quickly get complicated because the promise of design education (hereinafter thee Promise) is not unambiguously formulated—there is no clear contract—and yet it looms over the promisee, serving both as encouragement and threat. It may be rooted in notions like success, career, self-realization, ambition, or autonomy, but it may also aim to redefine them. It is affected by geography, class, race, and gender. It comes in multiple shapes and forms, and yet it can be understood as a whole. Does the Promise resemble a vow, an oath, a resolution, or a mission? Is it as nebulous and frail as the American dream? In the design field, things get even more complicated, as the field itself is at a perennial reconfiguration stage: it experiences a constant identity crisis, some might say, fueling the personal identity crises of its practitioners.

Focusing on the Promise means bridging pre-existing societal conditions—such as employability, welfare, housing availability, discrimination, mobility, and privilege—with socialized professional and personal aspirations: lifestyle, institutional roles, the legacies of crafts, research trends, urgent matters, subcultures, or notions of virtuosity. In other words, the Promise is built on certain premises, at once both materialistic and idealistic. When there is no full alignment between a promise and its premises, the promisee feels they are compromising. From this arises a question: who is defaulting when the Promise is not fulfilled? And what may be demanded by way of compensation?

Acknowledging the Promise means foregrounding intimate confessions, atmospheric peer pressure, individual anguish, tacit dissatisfaction, concrete limitations, but also creating hacks, finding new paths, imagining different ways of living and working. It means reflecting on the design field's linguistic tics and automatisms (such as working "at the intersection between") in order to forge new vocabularies and approaches. It means designing new alignments of personal goals, collective aspirations and societal conditions.

IMAGINATION

The first chapter of C. Wright Mills's 1959 book *The Sociological Imagination* is entitled "The Promise." This chapter is not, as I suspected, about generic expectations, such as having a house, finding a job, or building a career. What Mills talks about is "the promise of social science," ensured by a fundamental skill that the social scientist should muster.

The skill in question is the sociological imagination. It is about connecting the personal and the societal, what Mills calls "the interplay of man and society, of biography and history, of self and world." It consists in understanding personal troubles in the light of structural issues. A problem for Mills is any adequate formulation of these two scales. This is how he discusses it:

> The sociological imagination enables its possessor to understand the larger historical scene in terms of its meaning for the inner life and the external career of a variety of individuals.

It enables him to take into account how individuals, in the welter of their daily experience, often become falsely conscious of their social positions. Within that welter, the framework of modern society is sought, and within that framework the psychologies of a variety of men and women are formulated. By such means the personal uneasiness of individuals is focused upon explicit troubles and the indifference of publics is transformed into involvement with public issues. The first fruit of this imagination—and the first lesson of the social science that embodies it—is the idea that the individual can understand his own experience and gauge his own fate only by locating himself within his period, that he can know his own chances in life only by becoming aware of those of all individuals in his circumstances. In many ways it is a terrible lesson; in many ways a magnificent one.

As we can see, situatedness is crucial to the understanding of how certain values might be cherished or threatened, and how we react to such encouragements or threats. Mills provides a spectrum of reactions: well-being, indifference, anxiety, and panic. These collective reactions are what he calls trends. What we are attempting here, bearing in mind Mills's terribly magnificent lesson, is to reflexively turn the lens of sociological imagination to the milieu of (graphic) design, by looking at the implicit promises of design education. For a start, we might simply paraphrase some of Mills's questions: What varieties of [practitioners] now prevail in this field and in this period? And what varieties are coming to prevail? In what ways are they selected and formed, liberated and repressed, made sensitive and blunted?

THE SCHOOL

Undoubtedly, the design field is vast and diverse, and so are design schools. What I want to focus on here is the kind of design school that is not uncomfortable with being associated with art: by hinting at the fruitful relationships between the fields and their historical entanglement (think of the tradition of applied arts), I am more interested in the design schools that belong to the art academy than in those associated with architectural or engineering departments. This doesn't fully solve our framing problem, though. So my strategy will be to consider not a singular institution, and not even a series of them. Instead, I will focus on the School. The School is an "ideal type," a useful fiction that—for the sake of argument—combines, isolates (and maybe exaggerates) traits of the actual institutions I have observed via personal involvement or distant scrutiny. Whereas the Promise is real, albeit vague, the School is unreal and yet based on real-life cases.

These cases, which are concentrated largely in the urban hubs of the Netherlands (as well as being linked with the UK and the United States) are definitely a minority and don't represent design education as a whole. However, they perceive themselves—and are often perceived—to be a sort of avant-garde. Embodying newness, the School appears to offer paths to other organizations, both educational and professional. Perhaps supported by a generous system of public funding, the School may legitimately consider itself a site of reflection, cultural production, and renovation. Admittedly, its novel culture is not passively accepted by the field at large—indeed, it is often confuted, adverted, or simply ignored. And yet this culture influences the design field. Whereas the School has the means to make a cultural idea visible to the field, it is not hegemonic and does not wish to be, at least ostensibly. The School does not say "design should be this or that," but it presents itself as the locus of doubt and experimentation. Certain ideas developed within the School will leak out into the field at large, through the practices of its alumni, through final shows, through textual production and debates, hopefully to be later cemented into the course of design history. It might even do so through the mockery, skepticism, and disdain of its detractors. In a 2011 essay, Rob Giampietro pointed out that the culture of design was becoming increasingly like the culture of the school. The School is the testbed where this very equivalence is produced. So, turning the postulate around, talking of the School means talking of the culture of design.

BIOGRAPHY

In the same essay, Giampietro wonders how the attitude of designers is formed. This question was triggered by something that he noticed in the context of design schools: an emphasis on biographies and a heightened sense of self-awareness. The author points out that this biographical focus is not the result of a narcissistic leniency but that it may be interpreted as one of the main burdens of the modern subject. As sociologist Ulrich Beck stated, "people are condemned to individualization."

Being proudly international, the School values and encourages biographical expression as an interface to cultural difference, a badge of honor given its multicultural ethos. However, the risk is that a biography perceived as uncommon—in geographical, class, or bodily terms—might be exoticized and therefore "othered" once again. Here, the unfamiliar biography is made valuable ("one's roots") not for its intrinsic value as the story of a life but because of its rarity. A work that mobilizes an unfamiliar life story is framed as a cultural statement while one that is rooted in a relatively common biography might be deemed mere egotistic indulgence. Not everyone's "becoming who they are" is validated in the same way. In both cases, the School is in trouble because it struggles to discern the biographical from the personal, what it relates to one's place in society from what is a feature of individual character, what is debatable from what should be unquestionable.

A keyword that points to such tensions is *position*. The most frequent question one hears in the School is: "How do you position yourself?" The question is of course one of a maieutic kind: it is meant to help students situate themselves in the issue they are investigating or, more rarely, in the problem they're trying to solve (more on that later). The question works as an injunction because it forces the student to produce—or at least reflect on—a self-image. The position might be the one of the designer as mediator, as problem-solver, as activist, etc. Or more broadly, for instance, as male, as Western, as able-bodied. Positional complexities now lie at the heart of the field's identity crisis. As the School as a whole rarely has the conceptual tools to address them, this identity crisis (that has always characterized the field and now just feels more apparent) is shared with, if not offloaded onto, the student-practitioner.

What is the School's responsibility here? Will it still be able to reproduce itself as a progressive institution? How can it facilitate the generative crisis of the field without turning it into the identity crisis of individual students? Positional maieutics is a valid and useful medium, but the dilemmas and wicked problems it engenders should not be merely outsourced to individual students. Furthermore, the School should use those dilemmas neither as formal nor informal evaluation criteria, such as a grade or the conferral of trust.

AUTONOMY

The very fact that one can reflect on and to an extent shape one's position suggests that the Promise is one of autonomy and self-discovery. However, this process is rarely linked to material constraints. When urging students to become who they are, the School develops alertness and sensitivity only partially: it is rarely concerned with class, census, or wealth. Any talk on professional exploitation and self-exploitation, increasingly high fees, low pay, unemployment, unfair working conditions, uneven funding possibilities, expiring visas, etc.—in one word, precarity—is still infrequent. As it is infrequent to point the finger at the most obvious power imbalance within educational institutions: on the one hand, the almighty managerial class (the stable organogram) and on the other, the fragile teaching staff, whose members are occasional and on the verge of redundancy. Instead, successful stories imbued with survivorship bias 1 Cf. https://en.wikipedia.org/wiki/Survivorship_bias are foregrounded.

To avoid misunderstandings, let me say this loud and clear: all dimensions of inequality are equally important. Not just important: they are real and inextricably linked. A School that is explicitly anti-racist and non-patriarchal is also, by default, against precarity. If that thing we call progress actually exists, this is where we see it. And an emphasis on precarity is very much needed as it counterbalances the myth of life and career self-determination that can be fueled by a simplistic idea of autonomy and self-direction. Emphasis on inequality would foreground what is statistically hard to achieve and what aspects of practice are strictly dependent on local possibilities. In other words, to what extent society determines one's biography.

I suspect that any shortsightedness towards professional limitations arise from design and designers' sense of protagonism (and more rarely, from a solid and remunerative career). What matters is the mark the designer leaves on the world, not the scar that the world leaves on the designer. Professional disadvantage might sound gloomy, depressing, almost a petty subject. A workshop on precarity? Doesn't sound fun. Surely the School doesn't want to sadden its students? And yet, workshops on entrepreneurship abound. Is there a way to direct students' attention to these topics without curbing their enthusiasm? This is the dilemma that the School, usually so proud of its criticality, must address if it wants to be considered fully critical.

PRACTICE

The promise of autonomy implies the principle of self-direction: within the School, students are given a space and time to direct their own work. A practice is the outcome of self-direction. What do we mean by that? "Practice" is a term used mainly in the arts to define an artist's poetics. It involves the artist's concerns, their method, their medium, and even their theoretical and ethical grounding. Through the decades, design has been considered a style, a craft, a method, and later a thinking approach. Now, with the notion of practice, we observe an extension of the meta-understanding of the designer's activity. What does this shift mean? Borrowing from programming, one might say that each "constant" of the discipline (method, technique, media and products, literacy, topics, ethical issues) may be turned into a "variable." Inevitably, a degree of specificity is lost as the student is encouraged to tweak all these variables. But if none of them is shared among peers, how can we call this a field? Again, the liberating potential of tweaking the very terms of one's work might also lead to isolation and individualization. The School, partially aware of this, compensates for this atomizing drive with participatory and collaborative modes of interaction.

I can't but wonder whether the practice model —with its consonance to the profoundly isolating subject formation of the art world, which rarely offers more than a faint sense of belonging—is a weak form of professional, and therefore social, reproduction. Maybe the traditional medium-based or problem-based orientation was stronger for the simple fact that it shared at least a number of fixed variables. The point, however, is not to choose one model over the other, but to raise a specific concern: what effects does the "practice of practices" have on identification? Is the School partially responsible for the disintegrating sense of belonging and tangible social isolation that many practitioners, often self-defined as "outsiders", feel? By offering an abstract promise of autonomy, is the School uncritically abdicating its role in order to nurture the field?

PROBLEM

Variable manipulation is so radical that one variable may take the place of the other. As Giampietro points out, in certain design contexts, "research […] is not only an analytic method but also a cultural product unto itself." The School presents research as the very artifact that is offered to the public. 2 Note added in 2025. See Claire Bishop's "Information Overload" (Artforum, 21 September 2023) for a historical overview of this approach in the art field and the author's critical assessment of it. However, it rarely clarifies what research actually means, who the recipient/consumer of the research is. The specter of self-referentiality rears its head: will this research be read and seen by designers only—and perhaps not even by them? The emancipating image of a practice "without reliance on commissions" and with no problem to solve might look like a cry into the void, just as the lack of commission might coincide with the absence of an audience. The sites in which research is consumed as a cultural product are mostly educational in ambition: the gallery, the museum, the School itself. It seems that the School is trapped in its own pedagogical afflatus, and extends the student paradigm to the public as a whole, a public that is often indifferent to it. Instead of the socially oriented "double commission" (the client and the public), we end up with a "zero commission": no public and no client.

Traditionally, problem solving has been a defining aspect of the design field. The designer used to solve problems, great and small. Perhaps pushed by the tedium and frustrations of client-based work and the scarcity of grand-scale problem-solving positions available, various currents have challenged this approach. As a consequence, the School has developed an allergy to that word: problem-solving feels petty and naïve, undignified. Designers are meant not to solve but to frame problems, in other words, to be cultural agitators, people who raise awareness: "influencers." Design's main mandate was once "the problem to solve"; now it is "the problematic issue to address." Is this an attempt to question the way problems are constructed by the system as a whole, or is it a form of disciplinary surrender?

Take Victor Papanek's complex diagrams of interrelations for an "integrated design team": one feels dizzy just looking at them. The reason these diagrams feel overwhelming is that they demand a configuration that hardly exists. Papanek provocatively asserted that the "minimal" design team would include social and behavioral sciences, math, biology, maybe even computer science (and also, commendably, the end users of the design). Outside of corporations and big studios, such a design team is mostly utopian. But the School, despite training designers who will frequently develop small-scale practices, operates according to this pseudo-fiction. As a result, students are forced to become their own minimal design team, timidly approaching all the disciplines involved. Since getting in touch with an expert is apparently effortless ("just drop her an email"), interviews and surveys (if and when the expert replies) become the interface with other areas of knowledge. Even before having a job, the student becomes "hyperemployed" (Bogost 1993).

The notion of scale is key. Papanek's not-so-minimal team is mainly economically viable when it comes to large-scale products and services, but the School's non-commercial autonomous practitioners rarely deal with them. Here's a depressing truth: for all the talk about design's role in society, the large-scale impact on the world left by designers as a demographic cohort lies less in the design work they do than in the consumer choices they make. The laptop they buy counts more than the poster they design with it.

Let us consider another of Papanek's diagrams, which states that the designer's share of a certain problem is rather small. In the interplay between these two diagrams lies the cognitive dissonance present in the School: the student is encouraged to explore the whole pyramid while being aware that they will mostly be confined to its tip or, more realistically, to its base. The scope may feel exciting and liberating at first, but also turn tiring and disorienting.

Here, a necessary distinction must be made between an educational context and the outside world.

The School offers a safe space for systems think-ing—an invaluable exercise from which the stu-dent undoubtedly benefits. But there is also a more worrisome consequence. It takes the form of an-ti-solutionist nihilism: problems are too big, multi-layered and wicked to even attempt to solve them, and so all we can offer is interpretation by means of critique, Frankfurt School-style. A critique that —it pains me to say this—is sometimes mired in con-formism and superficiality. A critique that seems to take morbid pleasure in portraying its object. A cri-tique that, as said before, rarely reaches a public any wider than the designer's own crowd. We should ask ourselves: what degree of agency do these modes of inquiry provide? Where are they supposed to land? Are there environments which are receptive to such approaches? If so, how can we nurture them? And are we able to identify locally situated problems that speak to broader systemic issues?

The modernist tradition of design was tied to a god-view perspective. The designer would observe the world from above. Now, the grand meta-scale of the problems tackled by the School perversely renews such perspective, but the sight couldn't be more different. Modernist universal values turn into the School's *reductio ad absolutum*: designers are now urged to engage *directly* with the megamachine, the hyper-object, the Stack… with Capital itself. This novel synoptic view resists synopsis: unlike in the past, it no longer shows the illusion of an orderly terrain, but a stormy sky heaving above a frightened practitioner. This scenario might have contributed to the emergence of the counter-currents of design intimism ("the world is scary: I'll just focus on myself") and even design revanchism, the latter mostly performed on Twitter ("design is useless: I want revenge").

The stormy sky is not just theoretical dramatization. Reality is indeed complex and multifaceted. In a word, scary. The School shouldn't deny this, but it must be able to provide guidance. It should attempt to bridge the scales, showing how the macro lies in the micro. It should resist the grandiose General Theory, but also prevent any defeating relativism. The role of the School should be to make large-scale things approachable and small-scale gestures valorized.

EXPERTISE

"'In the beginning was Design', obviously, but not industrial design," wrote Papanek. Designers argue that everything can be design, only then to reclaim their monopoly over it. Through the decades, this generalization took on another form: design became understood as a sort of glue between disciplines, a bit like cybernetics. As a result, designers started to see themselves as mediators, facilitators, interpreters… What of the vocabulary needed to fulfill such roles? I won't even bother—the list would be too long and controversial. But what I want to point out here is a double movement: on the one hand, designers trying to become polyglots to communicate with various experts, while on the other, relinquishing any intimate relationship with specific crafts. This is not just the outcome of the field's volition but also an aftereffect of the digital banalization of competences, e.g. typographic knowledge being crystallized in software.

Deskilling, which is another name for superficial overskilling (knowing a little bit of everything), goes hand in hand with softskilling. The designer is no longer an expert on crafts, processes, and methods but on mediation, articulation, and framing. Their environment is the meeting room and the conference panel rather than the laboratory or the studio. Their main medium: the slide deck or the video essay. 3 Note added in 2025. As well as the prompt. Here, we find a parallel with the tertiarization of work, where soft skills—both social and managerial—trump the hard skills of craft and making (in this respect, the overuse of the term "empathy" in service design comes to mind). At best, this may be seen as an intellectually rich interdisciplinary frontier; at worst, it might appear as a cerebral post-medium, post-craft territory. All of this takes place with the backdrop of a more general crisis of competence: experts are no longer to be trusted. Papanek called for an anti-specialized design education. In his view, the problem was "too much design" in the curricula. Four decades later, the School has indeed become a school of generalists, but I'm afraid he would consider much of what is produced there "'self-indulgent' anti-design."

Within this epochal change, the School rightly encourages the student to exercise care and considerateness, as well as to organize and facilitate the work and the hard skills of others, to become a sort of impresario who holds a vision. Next to this explicit level of valorization, there is also an implicit one where other soft skills matter: enthusiasm, proactivity, confidence, resilience, and flexibility. This begs the question of how considerate the School is itself toward those who do not fully adhere to the attitudinal norm it sets.

A student meme reads: "I went to art school and all I got was this fucking attitude." I find the attitudinal emphasis at the expense of craft a bit disconcerting. I'm afraid that the soft-skill, post-craft ideology of the School might in fact be rooted in entrepreneurship, or even worse, in outsourcing. In fact, it is not infrequent for students to use online marketplaces like fiverr.com to complete their projects. The general devaluation of skill specificity is also worrisome because, in a society that cherishes work above all, craft is often one of the few stable forms of identity-making: the mastery of a craft goes way beyond a professional title. "A good job well done (Sennett 2009) can provide an anchor of personal stability within an ocean of impostor syndrome and self-doubt. Furthermore, craft goes against radical, make-believe horizontalism by showing the positive side of hierarchy: a workshop master–apprentice relationship is not in itself an exploitative, abusive one.

POLITICS

A semiotician once told me: "Design schools train students to become whatever they want, except designers." Given what might be considered as an expansion (or even a dilution) of the design field, the School can no longer be seen mainly as a site of professional reproduction but rather as a forge of attitude. The School allows the student to manifest their cultural and subcultural interests, their hobbies, their *nerditude*. Part of the Promise lies is the opportunity to transform all these identity features into a project portfolio. To turn cultural consumption into cultural production, cultural capital into economic capital. There's nothing wrong with that, but it is a development worthy of reflection. Shall we call it the adolescent turn? After all, the design field is kind of young. Adolescence is self-referential by definition: it is more about the self than the world. And anyone who used to wear a RATM t-shirt during their teenage years knows that politics is one of the various forms of identity-building.

The School actively encourages this form of identification: being "political" is a plus. There is, however, an idea of politics which I find slightly reductive: politics in terms of what the work *says* more than what it *does*. The statement, the manifesto, the invective are more positively scrutinized than the inner logic or the social relationality of a work. Politics as a badge rather than a process, with the further risk of turning it into a fetish, a formal requirement, or a norm. The design field at large is still imbued with ornamental politics (Lorusso 2018): the radical slogan, the activist posture, the glorious declaration are adopted as decorations of purely autonomous practices, i.e. cut off from the murky waters of micro- and macro-politics. Often—though not always—the political is reduced to the equivalent of a Che Guevara pin on a Fjällräven Kånken backpack.

In 1998, Mister Keedy wrote in the pages of Emigre: "Today's young designers don't worry about selling out, or having to work for 'the man,' a conceit almost no one can afford anymore. Now everyone wants to be 'the man.' What is left of an avant-garde in graphic design isn't about resistance, cultural critique, or experimenting with meaning. Now the avant-garde only consists of technological mastery: who is using the coolest bit of code or getting the most out of their HTML this week." In the context of the School, quite the opposite is true: explicit cultural critique comes at the expense of "mastery," which is deemed a form of narrow-mindedness. I'm not saying that the School should reject politics and pretend to be neutral, because we know there is no such thing as political neutrality. What I'm saying is that political orientations shouldn't become a passepartout. The student should not be pushed to inject politics for politics' sake into the work. And politics should be understood broadly: a political work, understood as a work with explicit politics, is not superior to a "formal" work, one which deploys its politics implicitly.

INFORMALITY

The School resists formal structures, and it even conspires against them. Within its environment, a suspension of disbelief towards formality is produced: the School is in denial of the very fact that it is indeed a formal institution. Somehow, it has digested decades of self-organized educational initiatives. The School conceives itself as an anti-school, a parallel school, a site of unlearning and relearning. This self-image is part of the allure it emanates and the spirit it projects. Informality doesn't just come naturally but is the product of protean intentionality, corroborated by a broader distrust of bureaucratic structures. Yet this informal turn goes hand in hand with an inflation of managerialism, which is a type of bureaucracy that is able to mobilize informality. Being put to work, informality becomes the School's new formalism.

Designer and writer Jacob Lindgren (2020) recently published a piece in which he criticizes the rigid structure of current graphic design schools. "We need the common, the occupied, the appropriated, and the lesser governed spaces," Lindgren writes, quoting "A Letter for the Academy" by Parallel School. This could well have been a statement issued by the School itself. Informality doesn't like numbers, it prefers words—only certain words actually, and "student" is not among them. Instead of grades, it generates a multiplication of feedback forms and conversations. Despite wanting to be holistic and horizontal, informality does not erase the intrinsic power imbalance between teachers and students (and even more, that between teachers and management). New forms of validation—no less messy and abstract and obscure than grades—emerge: individualized collaboration opportunities, good words, friendships. Validation becomes interpersonal rather than institutional. Charm acquires prominence. Emotion work becomes at least as important as productive labor. Governing forces feel *too human* to bear.

Validation also affects the teaching staff, partially fueling the Promise. The School's teachers (often called "coaches" or "mentors") are generally practitioners as well: they're able to make a living out of their practice, or so it appears at least. While teaching, they are also substantiating their research. Sometimes, it is the very income derived from teaching that makes their professional persona possible and, thus, real. As students logically aspire to build such a professional persona for themselves, the School, like an ouroboros, offers the Promise of itself. To what extent is this form of validation in line with that of the industry and society at large? To avoid "no grades" turning into "no jobs," the continuous effort to bridge validation systems—both internal and external, implicit and explicit—should be one of the School's main concerns.

This is not to say that the student is uninfluential or uncritical. It might well be that a generation of students develops a wariness towards the kind of persona that the School encourages. There is a metabolic relationship between the School and the student. The former exerts explicit or implicit power on the latter, while the latter influences and reshapes the former, bringing new conceptual energy to it. While the opaqueness of validation is the downside of informality, an ease of reconfiguration is its upside.

FUTURE

To what extent is the School actually attentive to the future? The temporally and geographically distant, and therefore safe, canned futures of speculation are favored over the tedious and mundane present-like pseudo-future of life-after-graduation. Again Papanek: "It is also in the interest of the Establishment to provide science-fiction routes of escape for the young, lest they become aware of the harshness of that which is real." As this prospect is grim in the most unspectacular way (this is what makes it terrifying), 4 Note added in 2025. Rereading this passage made me think of Simone Weil: "Imaginary evil is romantic and varied; real evil is gloomy, monotonous, barren, boring. Imaginary good is boring; real good is always new, marvelous, intoxicating." the School recasts the Promise as something oriented to the present: a promise of space and time, sheltered from the idiotic frenzy of the daily grind. In fact, many students arrive at the School *after* years of professional activity.

An orientation toward the present makes sense: if the School is truly a site of cultural production, what it has to offer are mostly the relationships that take place under its umbrella. Thus, not cultural production but the production *of a* culture. Some would call this "prefigurative politics," a sort of controlled experiment that is meant to be implemented later on a broader societal scale. If this is the case, the issue of individual sustainability should be central. On exiting the sandbox, will the student tumble into the abyss?

This is the humble urgency that even students themselves tend to put off to the final months of their education (if they are not preoccupied with things like visas), in favor of more epic and apparently noble urgencies, dictated by the agenda of the museum-festival complex. One does not even have to wait for graduation to encounter the unfashionable urgency of circumstances, as proved by the crowdfunding campaigns to afford to conclude one's studies in cities with sky-high rent and a housing crisis, or even to begin these studies in the first place! A new "design challenge" is gaining traction: craft a GoFundMe to sustain your design studies in a fancy cultural hub.

THE FIELD

To conclude, let us to go back to Mills's paraphrased question: What varieties of [practitioners] now prevail in this field and in this period? And what varieties are coming to prevail? In what ways are they selected and formed, liberated and repressed, made sensitive and blunted?

In this text, I tried to problematize a series of developments in design education. I focused on my own niche context, but I suspect students and educators outside of it will recognize many of the issues I dealt with. Among them, the ascendance of a biographical style. I provided various interpretations for it: a way to stabilize oneself within increasing complexity and professional dilution; a problematic interface for cultural diversity; an intimate disengagement from the world; an identity-making process based on the mobilization of a certain cultural or subcultural capital, and finally, a form of self-indulgence.

It is risky for an educational organization to engage with biography, especially in a time when individualism is thrust upon individuals. Not every facet of biography should be scrutinized by the School. And the ones who deserve attention should not be personalized. To manage this complexity, the School should become able to navigate intimacy, privacy, and confidentiality. Most of all, it should avoid flattening a life story into the project-practice surface for evaluation or promotional purposes.

The Promise has to do with the design of the self. Self-design can be umbilical, pathologically self-reflexive, and asocial. It can be unsettled by an essence that is not there. It can obsessively measure itself up against the ghost of identity. This is its recurring theme. Hence, it is not hard to understand the desperation of those students who come to school to engage with a system of thought, and instead find themselves placed in front of a mirror.

Through self-design, biography relates to the notion of autonomy (might we then, with autofiction in mind, speak of *autodesign* instead?). But autonomy can mean exile. Self-direction can lead to isolation. The variable-tweaking process that constitutes design practices might resemble micro-targeting in advertising: as specific as to address one person only. It might be that "at the intersection of" (an expression commonly found in designers' bios) there is no one else but you. Autonomy can adumbrate precarity and insidiously replicate that much-despised design protagonism. In which case, that is not autonomy but wishful thinking. *Fauxtonomy*, if you will.

Modernist comfort might be gone for good, but postmodern disorientation is here to stay. Complexity looms over us. What are we to make of ourselves? Identity crises are not just personal: they exist on many scales. The presentiment of mundane futurelessness is concealed by the glamor of Big Dystopia. Tempted by the dilution of over-skilling and mesmerized by the frontier of multidisciplinarity, avant-garde design education might be disseminating existential self-doubt and confusion at the cost of professional reproduction and solid identity-making.

To avoid succumbing to the multilayered identity crises driven by fauxtonomy and futurelessness, it's time to put self-design aside and rebuild the field. The field is the space inhabited by a series of connected communities of practice 5 Cf. https://en.wikipedia.org/wiki/Community_of_practice (where practice is *not* understood as it is in contemporary art, namely devoid of any authentic communal sense). The field does not shy away from problems. Instead, it constantly redefines its own set of issues and concerns: functional issues, ethical issues, issues of method, of access, of inclusion. The field deals with complexity but does not attempt to tackle it in its entirety. 6 Note added in 2025. Donna Haraway building upon Thom Van Dooren: "Nobody lives everywhere; everybody lives somewhere. Nothing is connected to everything; everything is connected to something." Through the specialized knowledge it produces and the situated activity it performs, it glances at complexity without being blinded by its frightening, god-like appearance.

The field is a political entity, but not because it regularly issues statements and manifestos (although it might do that as well). The field is political insofar as it is concerned with its own organizational politics, as well as the politics of the artifacts it designs and circulates. The field is preoccupied with tangible, lower-case futures. The future lies in its surroundings but also in the broader effects that interventions on these surroundings have. It is thus embedded in a gradient of scales.

The field is not a scene: its main driving force is not visibility. It might even unconsciously limit exchanges with the outside world. But if it becomes too self-referential, that's not the field: it's a club. The main interface with the outside and between its members is a physical space: the field is aware of the insufficiency of online-only communication.

The field is not a school: while learning takes place within it, scholastic hierarchies—both implicit and explicit—don't apply there. This doesn't mean that it rejects hierarchy completely: its structure is based on the healthy, reconfigurable hierarchies of apprenticeship, amateurship, and curiosity.

The field isn't a school and the School isn't the field, but they mutually benefit from each other (collaborations with local collectives, self-organized spaces, etc.). What the School gains from the field is a sense of specificity and purpose; what the field gets from the School is financial resources and the possibility to open up to new publics. But the exchange is asymmetrical. The field stands in a less stable position: collectives come and go, and their sustainability is constantly put to the test. The occasional workshop fee is not enough to keep the field alive. And yet, given its ambitions and limitations, the School is increasingly dependent on a lively field. Without the energies of a surrounding field, the School is doomed to become a managerial graveyard.

The field is informal in nature, but it doesn't fetishize informality: it resists character normativity and protects its people from hurtful behavior. The field is attentive to its flows of social, cultural, and economic capital: it is generous with quoting, crediting, and remunerating; it doesn't trust impresarios or creative directors; it rejects inner qualitative distinctions: all the work it needs is essential, interdependent work. Validation comes with effort,

helpfulness, and mutuality, more than with smart-
ness, talent, and bravado. The field is not a guild:
it's not preoccupied with the protection of its trade.
The field believes in expertise, but it doesn't wor-
ship experts.

The field provides an activity-based sense of belonging and identity: people have roles and purposes,
but these may be renegotiated. The field understands
biographical and cultural differences, but foregrounds them only when necessary. In a thriving field,
practitioners can joyfully forget about themselves.

Bogost, Ian. "Hyperemployment, or the Exhausting Work of the Technology User." *The Atlantic*, November 8, 2013.

Giampietro, Rob. "School Days." *Line & Unlined*, 2012 https://linedandun-
lined.com/archive/school-days/

Keedy, Mr. "Graphic Design in the Postmodern Era." *The AIGA National
Student Design Conference*, CalArts, June 14, 1998.

Lindgren, Jacob. "Graphic Design's Factory Settings." *Walker Reader*, January 2, 2020.

Lorusso, Silvio. "The Designer Without Qualities – Notes On Ornamental
Politics, Ironic Attachment, Bureaucreativity and Emotional Coun-
terculture." *Institute of Network Cultures*, January 19, 2018.

Sennett, Richard. *The craftsman*. London: Penguin Books, 2009.

Slightly revised version of an essay written in 2020. Excerpts were published in *Who Can Afford to Be Critical?*, edited by Afonso de Matos (Set
Margins', 2022), and included in the book *What Design Can't Do* (Set Margins', 2023). My gratitude goes to Manetta Berends, Sami Hammana, Geert
Lovink, and Gui Machiavelli for reading drafts of this text and giving precious feedback. I'm also thankful to Varia (varia.zone), which represents in
many ways the community of practice I tend to idealize here. This work is
the result of countless discussions, disagreements, and misunderstandings
with students and colleagues. I wish to thank them all. I do so anonymous-
ly as I don't wish the School to be understood as a school in particular: it is
not. Each school exceeds the School because actual human relationships
are ineluctably exceptional and unique.

Nida Abdullah
Making Anyway, as Undergrowth

From the entangled position of teaching, research-ing, and making, I witness institutions as colonial technologies, perpetuating systems that transform living knowledge into property. By institution and institutional, I mean not just organizations, not just buildings, but the sets of rules, programs, and proce-dures that shape what can be known and how. This institutional form is always already colonial, insep-arable from the logics of capture and containment. These "mechanisms of maintenance" are the ongo-ing operations of colonial epistemology (Rizvi 2024): they capture, translate, or eliminate what cannot be governed. Recognition becomes an administrative tool, converting diverse ways of knowing into insti-tutional currency that can be catalogued, owned, and then exchanged. These forms acquire their shape through repeated actions that orient bodies and knowledges toward logics of possession and control (Ahmed 2012). Inclusion becomes conscription, where being recognized means being made legible to the very systems that require containment.

This maintenance is epistemological violence (Spivak 1988) in its most refined form: transforming fluid knowledge into bordered property, movement into stasis, relation into commodity. What the colo-nial archive could not contain through direct vio-lence, contemporary institutions subsume through recognition.

To refuse legibility is therefore to enact epistemic disobedience (Mignolo 2010), rejecting the colonial de-mand to be known on its own terms. Illegibility and opacity become modes of resistance that maintain what Édouard Glissant (1997) calls the right to opacity, the right not to be fully understood or translated on external terms. Like the institution, the archive operates through capture, while the repertoire opens up other ways of knowing. As Diana Taylor (2003) describes, the archive refers to what can be fixed in documents, objects, and collections, while the repertoire refers to knowledge carried in bodies, gestures, and relations that unfold over time. The archive holds and preserves, whereas the repertoire lives through repetition and transmission, constantly remade in the act of doing. This distinction matters here because repertoire undermines the authority of the archive and keeps knowledge alive in movement, in relation, and in practice. I locate my practice within this repertoire, within what I call the undergrowth: where embodied making explores how knowledge persists and refuses containment. Not something below, beneath or secondary, but something multi-dimensional, multi-temporal.

In my work, I center gota: a textile adornment material and practice which emerged in the pre-colonial Indian subcontinent. Working with inherited lineages of practices, materials, histories, bodies, and temporalities across imposed borders and boundaries, I examine how making with gota becomes both method and a kind of refusal. It is not gota itself but the working with it; expanding its possibilities, sharing stories through its making, connecting across violent divisions; this way of making enacts refusal. My practice navigates layered histories of British imperial rule through contemporary patterns of migration. Another colonial technology, partition, operates not as historical event, but as ongoing epistemic violence (Zamindar 2007); it represents the logic of extraction: the transformation of fluid practices into bordered property. Yet through making with gota, through the personal narratives that surface in its practice, I refuse these categorical impositions.

My making is a form of critical fabulation (Hartman 2008), not seeking to resolve or recover what has been lost, but to sit with fragments, to assemble without closure. Making, in this sense, is not solution-oriented but expansive. It opens rather than concludes, proliferates rather than consolidates. Through gota, I work with residues and inheritances not to reconstruct an authentic past or propose a corrective future, but to explore what forms in the space between the violences of partitioning and imposed borders, between hegemonic time and embodied duration, between what colonial modernity attempted to sever and what persists in gesture and practice. This is making as a practice of expanding possibility rather than answering questions, of holding multiple temporalities and truths without forcing them into legibility.

In 2023, I visited the Victoria and Albert Museum in London and encountered gota pieces acquired through colonial expansion and violence. I witnessed how institutional capture transforms living practice:

adornment textiles that once held complex layers of generational knowledge, meant to be worn and experienced, now sit static in cabinets, drawers, behind glass, their epistemological vitality converted into museum currency. What does this conversion make visible, and what does it erase? Where does the knowledge embedded in these materials persist, and how does it circulate beyond the frame of the museum?

Against this deadness, I think of working with my close friend Swati Piparsania. We exist on opposite sides of the India-Pakistan border, a line drawn to sever precisely these transmissions. In 2023 we worked together on an exhibition, but what materialized exceeded any documentary frame. Our practice moved at other speeds: slower, thicker, heavier. Knowledge growing dense between our hands: muscle memory recognizing itself across the partition, techniques passing between us without translation. We weren't performing heritage or recovering tradition. We were generating something else entirely, a frequency of practice that builds through time rather than display. Stories arose obliquely, refracted through the work itself, our mothers' ways surfacing in our gestures, not just our mothers but an entire lineage of mothers, our grandmothers' knowledge transmitted through networks of women who taught each other through parallel practice, a collective intelligence that exceeds any individual inheritance. The exhibition could document the objects we made, but not this intelligence that moves between bodies, not the way in which making together creates its own temporal field, its own form of study that needs no institutional witness in order to be real.

This practice continues through other intimacies too. With my mother, gota becomes something else: less urgent, more playful. We make silly little things that are just for us, objects that will never be exhibited, never documented. As we work, stories surface: Lucknow, Karachi, Aligarh, geographies that exceed the borders drawn through them. Histories become present not simply as narrative but as rhythm, as the particular way she tensions thread, ways of knowing she inherited from her mother who inherited from hers. This is making at its most ordinary and most radical: how understanding builds between us through the regular act of sitting together, hands moving, a shared moving, a togetherness. Knowledge lives in the repertoire (Taylor 2003), in bodies and gestures: felt before it is seen, sensed before it is measured (Campt, 2017, 2023).

This is how I understand making as epistemic practice: it generates knowledge through doing, through repertoire rather than archive. This knowledge operates in the undergrowth, those spaces where practice flourishes because it remains undetected by colonial epistemologies. Like roots' systems that communicate through signals below ground, growing alongside and with each other, this embodied knowledge transmits at registers that institutional sensors cannot detect, cannot capture (Campt 2017, 2023).

It spreads laterally rather than reaching upward, proliferating horizontally through the undergrowth rather than breaking through into visibility. When stories and knowledges surface in this space, they do so along different axes, emerging into perception while remaining in dimensions that cannot be mapped. This surfacing is the undergrowth itself, not revelation but a different kind of presence. It dwells, hums in the space between the gestural and the material, in the ongoingness of practice rather than the moment of recognition. Making with gota becomes a practice of cultivating the undergrowth, not hiding from power but growing in dimensions it cannot perceive, growing these densities of relation and knowledge.

The undergrowth is not prescriptive, not a method to be taught or transmitted, but descriptive of something already happening wherever people develop their own grammars of relation, where knowledge thickens through syntaxes that refuse translation. Through the everyday rather than spectacular intervention, through the unremarkable repetition of practice, we continue: making together, making anyway, not to answer questions but to expand what remains possible.

Ahmed, Sara. 2012. *On Being Included: Racism and Diversity in Institutional Life*. Durham: Duke University Press.

Campt, Tina M. 2017. *Listening to Images*. Durham: Duke University Press.

Campt, Tina M. 2023. "Black Visuality and the Practice of Refusal." *Women & Performance: A Journal of Feminist Theory* 29 (1): pp. 9–25.

Glissant, Édouard. 1997. *Poetics of Relation*. Translated by Betsy Wing. Ann Arbor: University of Michigan Press.

Hartman, Saidiya. 2008. "Venus in Two Acts." *Small Axe* 12 (2): pp. 1–14.

Mignolo, Walter D. 2010. "Epistemic Disobedience and the Decolonial Option: A Manifesto." *Transmodernity: Journal of Peripheral Cultural Production of the Luso-Hispanic World* 1 (2): pp. 44–66.

Rizvi, Uzma Z. 2024. "In Service to Decolonization." In *Through Witnessing: Threading the Critiquing, Making, and Teaching of Design*, Nida Abdullah, Chris Lee, and Xinyi Li (eds.). Eindhoven: Set Margins Press.

Spivak, Gayatri Chakravorty. 1988. "Can the Subaltern Speak?" In *Marxism and the Interpretation of Culture*, Cary Nelson and Lawrence Grossberg (eds.), pp. 271–313. Urbana: University of Illinois Press.

Taylor, Diana. 2003. *The Archive and the Repertoire: Performing Cultural Memory in the Americas*. Durham: Duke University Press.

Zamindar, Vazira Fazila-Yacoobali. 2007. *The Long Partition and the Making of Modern South Asia: Refugees, Boundaries, Histories*. New York: Columbia University Press.

Kseniia (xè) Obukhova

Obukhova

*Becoming
a Feminist Killjoy
Designer:
Notes From
Someone Who's
Still figuring
It Out*

> Hope gives us a sense that another world is possible or that there is a point to a struggle.
>
> (Ahmed, 2024, p. 81)

On several occasions over the past few months, I've been invited to reflect on my journey as a designer. This request doesn't come easy to me. As designers, we're trained to craft perfect presentations for others, but when it comes to speaking from the personal, words often fail us. It was then that I decided to recall the origins of this journey and ask myself: *Why design?* Though no story can fully represent everyone's reasons for such a choice, tracing my own motivations made me realize that elements of my journey might resonate with others from my generation, with those who also found themselves in design school, perhaps for reasons they only truly understood much later. So what exactly drew me here, *what inspired me to pursue a career in design in the first place?*

Answering that question immediately brought to mind the reactions of my new (non-designer) friends the moment I first introduced myself as one. It always landed better than expected, which made me briefly question what they thought designers actually *do*. That, in turn, reminded me of how I myself pictured a designer back in my teenage years: wearing something thrifted, mismatched but strangely stylish, with a sketchbook or MacBook always at hand. In St. Petersburg, where I grew up, you'd find them on Rubinstein Street, in one of those underground cafés or repurposed lofts where they only played indie rock and served craft coffee and local cider. As a high school student, I loved spending time in those environments. And designers, who were natives there, gave the impression of having all the time in the world to be—*God forbid*—creative. They were the ones moving beyond the mainstream social norms and were just doing their artsy thing. Becoming a designer seemed like having a key to access the world of contemporary bohème, which, when you are seventeen years old and on the verge of deciding what your future will look like, sounded like quite an attractive trajectory. I guess this idea of design I have just described is precisely what some people still imagine when they hear me say "I am a designer." And, for some reason, that makes us look like people who have it all in the eyes of others.

While this might have been my teenage dream, I have to admit that it did not take me too long to realize that design was actually—*and unsurprisingly*—quite a regular profession, not only intertwined with, but deriving from everything that is wrong with contemporary neoliberal societies. What else should I have expected if my understanding of a designer was based on the cover of *Kinfolk* magazine? Years passed, and I learned that looks can be misleading. It was then that I started noticing what is hidden away behind beautifully crafted packages and perfectly polished catalogues: that design, as Victor Papanek already warned back in the 1970s, is too often used "in persuading people to buy things they don't need, with money they don't have, in order to impress others who don't care." Despite coming from a different era, his book cracked something open. Ten years ago, when critical perspectives in design education were definitely not a priority, reading Papanek suddenly helped me realize that design was not so innocent. A couple of classes on branding and marketing later, I figured out that I'm not interested in elaborating strategies on how to make the rich even richer and the poor even poorer. That's when I started to search for more purpose in my practice and set out on a journey to become a *feminist killjoy designer.*

Quite recently, the independent feminist scholar Sara Ahmed published a beautiful book entitled *The Feminist Killjoy Handbook*, presenting a collection of stories and reflections on the experience of being a feminist, an activist, and a killjoy. From Papanek to Ahmed, it turns out, there is a long and bumpy road a designer must travel. This particular book, as the author herself highlights, is a result of years of a collective effort by a group of killjoys critical of dominant paradigms and narratives, those responsible for constructing the feminist as a killjoy figure in the first place. In a way that seems more of a wake-up call, Ahmed invites us to join the movement where an alternative form of joy is celebrated: that which Judith Butler (2024) described as "a joy that comes from doing critical damage to what damages." Not simply a handbook, but rather a

—sometimes disturbing, but always reasonable— companion, this text is a source of personal and emotional teachings and guidelines for those willing to experience the killjoy existence themselves.

But why a feminist killjoy? While reading this handbook, it was surprising to observe how many of the killjoy truths that Ahmed comes out with are somehow exemplary to my experience of being a designer and an activist without me necessarily knowing I was one. Those same teenage years that formed my passion for hipster magazines were also imbibed with tensions and injustices that I felt I was at the center of. From the unfolding crisis of life on Earth—fueled by irreversible human-made damage—to the frightening inequalities laid bare both locally and globally, the rise of social media and its culture of attention-seeking, curated perfection, and perpetual FOMO, it all started to pile up. Add to that the unstable, increasingly authoritarian political climate of my home country, where freedom of speech and expression became optional luxuries, and the disorienting experience of solo migration under the watchful eye of bureaucratic institutions. Just to name a few cheerful ingredients. These first-hand tensions came out in the form of essential values that accompany me to this day and that formed my (killjoy) personality like nothing else.

Perhaps I viewed diving into the creative industry as an opportunity to do something I enjoyed so much that it would help me forget about the feeling of being responsible for the world going up in flames.

What if this was the actual reason that brought me into the profession—a form of *comforting hope*? Back then, creativity provided what they call in Italian a *valvola di sfogo*, a relief valve. It promised to be a space for my passions to thrive, for my personality to unfold in ways that other disciplines would not allow. But maybe the killjoy in me was too persistent to simply keep quiet. Once I encountered this comforting hope, I realized that it was not what I actually wanted: it was that kind of *stubborn hopelessness* that was driving me more than anything else. And in the end, embracing that killjoy nature meant reclaiming design not as an escape from the world in flames, but as a way to confront it—by politicizing my practice and asking who and what it serves. As Ahmed reminds us, sometimes it's the absence of joy that pushes us to create new forms of it:

> We widen, we loosen; we are building something. Our experiences of not being accommodated, not having our needs met, teach us what we need to do to build a more accommodating world. We listen to others, we ask how to address them, ask what they need, knowing that we need to be open at any moment in time for what we are creating to be reshaped when it does not allow somebody else in. We breathe life into arrangements when we know they can be changed and by trying to change them. And there can be joy in that, happiness even; we feel everything (Ahmed, 2024, p. 256).

The troublesome figure of the feminist killjoy in Ahmed's companion is introduced through a series of truths, maxims, commitments, and equations. One after another, these killjoy revelations interrupted my flow of reading, making me pause for a second and reflect on what they were actually getting at. They all serve a different purpose, and as a designer—*yet again*—I could not help but notice their assertive boldness, insistently demanding attention by claiming the physical space of the book page. Killjoy *truths* are "hard-worn wisdoms" that transpire from the killjoy existence itself, from the friction of confronting what everyone else might prefer to comply with so as to preserve the collective happiness. Killjoy *maxims* are calls to action that make this handbook sound like you are reading messages from your fictional feminist mother: "Become a feminist infection!"; "Stay unhappy with this world!" Then come killjoy *commitments*: "the wills and the won'ts," those encouraging promises about future possibilities that we, as feminist killjoys, give ourselves, even if changing the world seems delightfully naïve. These promises include being "willing to cause unhappiness" or "be inconvenienced" in situations that reproduce harm or injustice. And finally, we are introduced to killjoy *equations*, little formulas that expose absurd truths about society ironically, yet equally uncomfortably.

Some of them hit differently. Take this killjoy truth: "*Those who are not 'at home' in categories tend to know more about them.*" I was reminded of just how

long it takes—or rather, how impossible it feels—
to call oneself a designer. Spoiler: *I still don't*. Why?
Because a "real" designer is—as we all remember—
someone who's got it all: a sleek studio (probably
renovated by their architect-friend), a shelf of international awards, a seat on some design board, and,
of course, a permanent gig at some design school,
since forever. So no, it's not exactly easy to "feel at
home" in that category when your portfolio consists
mostly of studio photos of half-functional proto-
types and a printed copy of your thesis project, cre-
atively scanned at the last minute. And reclaiming
the title becomes even trickier when your practice
doesn't really fit into any traditional design box to
begin with. Let me explain.

The story takes place at a graduation show held
at the Faculty of Art and Design of the Free University of Bozen-Bolzano. I remember strolling around
the campus, looking at exhibits by my peers from
the Eco-Social Design course, when I overheard
a couple of design students commenting: "I don't
even understand why they are part of this faculty."

That was not an isolated comment. As a student representative, I was regularly confronted
—sometimes with genuine disbelief—by how nar-
row the definition of "design" could be, even within
the faculty itself. The Master's in Eco-Social Design
is a program that strives to radically rethink how
we live, produce, and relate, aiming for futures that
might actually be worth living in. It disrupts the con-
sumer- and profit-oriented joy of traditional design

education, making design a tool for enabling the change we want to see in the world. Yes, we are the killjoys of design. Often, the outcomes of our work consisted not of visual identities, products, or digital interfaces, but of ecological interventions, social campaigns, or public provocations. And yet, despite design's expansion into everything from policymaking to activism, educational institutions remain strangely devoted to their staid old categories. These boundaries persistently remind us who counts as a "real" designer, and who doesn't.

Indeed, it does not get any easier when you start a PhD titled "Redesigning Democracy." At that point, it is not just designers I have to explain myself to, but also policymakers and colleagues from the Social Sciences department, many of whom look genuinely confused when I mention that I come from a design background and now research participatory environmental governance. Ironically, I've also been told that Social Sciences is too broad a term, one that means everything and nothing at the same time. That's when I leaned back in my office chair and fully embraced the beauty of disciplinary vagueness—where, apparently, almost anyone can belong. So maybe—*just maybe*—there's something we designers could learn from that kind of openness and, as Danah Abdulla (2021) taught us, allow ourselves to perform some *disciplinary disobedience*.

And while today, defining the work I do under a single category feels harder and harder, I've just accepted that it simply cannot be confined within boundaries. What matters, instead, is the kind of *hopelessness* that drives your practice and the kind of *hope* it enacts.

By now, you have probably realized that embarking on the journey of a killjoy is no picnic. It is about leaving a safe haven—one of *blissful joy*—where you could have found peace with what damages, but instead decided to depart right in the middle of a storm in a hopelessly hopeful aspiration for a world that is somehow different. I agree: not everyone "can afford to be critical," as we are reminded by Afonso Matos (2022) and his fellow design students suspended between the will to stay critical and the need to pay rent. After all, we are all stuck in systems that thrive on extraction and profit. But that doesn't mean we should stop trying. Even if, as Ahmed warns us, "we need to be prepared for our own joy to be killed." Because if we don't try, we risk becoming exactly what the system expects: compliant with the categories that these systems impose. A killjoy, on the other hand, learns to sit with discomfort, to recognize complicity, to confront their own privileges. It's rarely fun. But I'm glad I signed up for it. And I think—even if she wouldn't fully get it (yet)—my younger self would be proud.

So, do you want to join?

Abdulla, D. (2021). "Disciplinary Disobedience. A Border-Thinking Approach to Design." In C. Mareis & N. Paim (eds.), *DESIGN STRUGGLES: Intersecting Histories, Pedagogies, and Perspectives* (pp. 227–241). Valiz. https://doi.org/10.47982/bookrxiv.34

Ahmed, S. (2024). *The Feminist Killjoy Handbook*. Allen Lane, Penguin Books.

Butler, J. (February 21, 2024). *Sara Ahmed and the Joys of Killjoy Feminism*. https://www.thenation.com/article/society/sara-ahmed-killjoy-feminism/

Matos, A. (ed.) (2022). *Who can afford to be critical? An inquiry into what we can't do alone, as designers, and into what we might be able to do together, as people*. Set Margins.

Papanek, V. (2022). *Design for the Real World: Human Ecology and Social Change* (3rd ed.). Thames & Hudson.

I would like to thank Weronika Kozak and Giulia Cordin for sharing their precious comments with me in preparing this text.

Noemi Biasetton
When the Wor(l)d Fails: On Design Education in a Faltering Reality

The question of language has long been central to modern philosophy, particularly in the twentieth century, when thinkers across various traditions began to treat language not merely as a representational system but as the ground for thought and action. In his *Tractatus Logico-Philosophicus*, 1 Ludwig Wittgenstein, *Tractatus Logico-Philosophicus* (Kegan Paul, Trench, Trubner & Co., 1922). Ludwig Wittgenstein famously proposed that language and the world are isomorphic—meaning that language functions as a logical mirror of reality, sharing its underlying structure. But in his later work, *Philosophical Investigations*, 2 Ludwig Wittgenstein, *Philosophical Investigations* (Basil Blackwell, 1953) he dismantles that view. Language, he argues, does not reflect the world: it constitutes it. Meaning is not fixed by logic or structure, but emerges from use—from context, from social life, from the messy entanglements of habit, gesture, and power.

This shift from language as a mirror to language as a practice paved the way for later thinkers—such as Derrida, Foucault, and Butler 3 Some of the texts that exemplify this shift include: Judith Butler, *Gender Trouble: Feminism and the Subversion of Identity* (Routledge, 2006); Jacques Derrida, *Of Grammatology* (Les Éditions de Minui, 1967); Michel Foucault, *L'archéologie Du Savoir* (Éditions Gallimard, 1969).—to explore how meaning is never innocent, but always contingent, performative, and embedded in power structures. For these theorists, language does not simply describe the world but *does* something: it shapes norms, constitutes subjects, and governs what can be said, felt, or imagined. Wittgenstein's attention to the ordinary, the contextual, and the unsayable thus resonates with critical theory's suspicion of totalizing systems and its focus on the unstable, contested terrain of discourse. In contemporary theory, what he called "forms of life" become the crucible where meaning is made and unmade.

In design theory, relatively few scholars have explored the deep interdependence between language and design practice. Design is often described metaphorically as a "language of its own," particularly in educational discourse. Nigel Cross, for instance, famously advocated for "designerly ways of knowing," 4 Nigel Cross, "Designerly Ways of Knowing," *Design Studies*, Special Issue Design Education, 3, no. 4 (October 1, 1982): 221–27, https://doi.org/10.1016/0142-694X(82)90040-0. framing design as a "third area" of education alongside science and the humanities. In this context, he likened design learning to acquiring an artificial language—"a kind of code which transforms 'thoughts' into 'words.'" 5 Ibid, p. 224. However, this metaphor tends to obscure the fact that design is never autonomous from language. If we follow Wittgenstein's insight that meaning is rooted in use within shared forms of life, then design must also be understood as embedded in (and dependent on) linguistic, cultural, and social practices. Every attempt to treat design as a language "of its own making" runs up against this deeper entanglement: design cannot escape the discursive structures through which meaning, value, and legitimacy are produced.

Among contemporary design theorists, Tony Fry stands out for confronting the entanglement between language, world-making, and design practice head-on. In his renowned book *Defuturing: A New Design Philosophy*, 6 Tony Fry, *Defuturing: A New Design Philosophy* (London: Bloomsbury Visual Arts, 2020). he argues that history itself is a "literary construction, from an always biased perspective, that translates various forms of historical materials into a usually academically validated narrative," 7 Ibid, p. 72. and that design history, in particular, occupies a marginal and under-theorized position within that landscape. To imagine alternative futures (in design and, more generally, in the world), he argues that we must engage in the "unmaking and remaking" of the very grounds of knowing and acting. 8 Ibid. This also and above all includes language, intended as the discursive habits, symbolic systems, and inherited categories that structure what can be thought, designed, or even perceived. As Fry writes, "we are the world we invent—it is both our project and our projection of meaning, it is our discourse—and it is nothing without us." 9 Ibid. Such a view aligns with Wittgenstein's insight that meaning is not fixed in things but arises through use, embedded in shared forms of life. It also echoes the critical theorists' understanding that language is never neutral, but rather shapes the contours of subjectivity, normativity, and futurity. Fry's call for an *ontological theory* of design (which he theorized as Design with a capital D) thus hints at a practice in which making and speaking, designing and theorizing, are inseparable.

As I write in mid-2025, we find ourselves surrounded by a new vocabulary that shapes our political and social realities. Terms like "post-truth" or "alternative reality" are well-embedded in our lexicon, with after over ten years from their first emergence; many more, like "rearmament," are slowly creeping in and becoming the norm; others like "genocide" or "post-fascism" still fail to make it to our "mainstream" understanding of the contemporary world, often relegated to "extreme" or "radical" views on the world. What bedazzles me, however, is the language that is supposed to "counteract" the real actions that these words perpetuate. Today, in fact, terms like "sustainability," "inclusivity," and "peace" circulate as hollow signals, fragments of a language that no longer holds the complexities of our world. They are repeated, repackaged, and turned into branding by most Western governments, preserving face value through strategic ambiguity while entire realities collapse beneath them. And, unfortunately, design is very much complicit in this dynamic.

If we are to understand design as a "powerful ontological tool capable of transforming the social and cultural reality, and modeling human experience, subjectivity and life style, and environment and social events," as famously described by Madina Tlostanova, then "design is clearly one of the spheres in which ontology, epistemology, and axiology intersect in a dynamic and creative way." 10 Madina

Tlostanova, "On Decolonizing Design," *Design Philosophy Papers* 15, no. 1 (January 2, 2017): 51, https://doi.org/10.1080/14487136.2017. 1301017. **In this sense, design is fully embedded within the crisis of language, and it manifests it through aesthetics that are never neutral and forms that are never innocent.** 11 On this topic see: Cheryl Buckley, "Made in Patriarchy: Toward a Feminist Analysis of Women and Design," *Design Issues* 3, no. 2 (1986): 3–14, https://doi.org/10.2307/1511480; Chris Lee, *Immutable: Designing History* (Onomatopee, 2022); Ruben Pater, *The Politics of Design: A (Not So) Global Design Manual for Visual Communication* (BIS, 2016). **Design is the ensemble of processes that construct infrastructures imbued with ideology as it mediates, translates, and legitimizes, smoothing over fractures through meticulous typography and speculative optimism. It builds futures no one asked for while disguising the present as inevitable. This is not a call for redemption, but a reminder that design is always a site of struggle, entangled in the very language that shapes our thoughts and slips from our tongues.**

Thus, the question that emerges from these reflections is how can design operate within this tension while acknowledging its capacity to simultaneously uphold and dismantle the Agambenian apparatuses 12 Agambenian apparatuses refer to the systems, structures, and mechanisms—ranging from institutions and technologies to language and social norms—that capture, govern, and subjectify living beings. Building on Foucault, Agamben emphasizes that apparatuses are not neutral tools but operate as forces that separate individuals from their potential, producing subjects aligned with dominant power structures. See: Giorgio Agamben, "*What Is* *an Apparatus?" and Other Essays* (Stanford University Press, 2009).

of everyday life. Especially when the very structures in which design discourse and practice are meant to be produced—schools and universities—are themselves embedded in strategic uses of language.

In fact, within many European academic and institutional learning environments, two familiar scenarios tend to unfold. On one hand, in schools where design education is celebrated for its "critical approach," the pedagogical structures through which this very "critical" knowledge is enacted often remain largely unchanged. In this way critical discourse is introduced, but delivered through institutional forms that reproduce the very conditions it seeks to challenge. Thus, the classroom becomes a space where radical content is discussed within conservative frameworks: students engage with decolonial theory, feminist epistemologies, and climate imaginaries—yet the teaching logic utilised to deliver that content remains anchored in Eurocentric, patriarchal, and productivist models. This contradiction fosters tension: critique is encouraged but rarely allowed to destabilize the system.

On the other hand, some schools prioritize the professionalization of students through client briefs and market-driven relevance, reducing design to a service function and aligning it tacitly with dominant economic and ideological systems. Even when experimental pedagogies are introduced—emphasizing collaboration, speculation, or interdisciplinarity—the outcomes often remain constrained by the expectations of capitalist logics: portfolios, deliverables, and employability.

To all of this, the political superstructures that govern European countries must be added, many of which are increasingly infiltrating academic discourse itself. I'm thinking in particular of the repression of student activism in support of the Palestinian cause—through censorship and intimidation 13 Noemi Biasetton, "In the 'Real World', Nothing Is Neutral: Design Schools, Conflict, and the Question of Palestine," *villardjournal* (forthcoming, 2025).—but also of the broader misalignment between faculty and students in many universities, where the latter feel their demands are not taken seriously into account by their teachers. This disconnect, which ultimately results in a power struggle, often prevents the emergence of a shared space for inventing a new vocabulary from which to (re) invent design practices.

And yet, in these tensions lie openings. Misalignments between what is taught and how, between theory and form, intention and infrastructure mark the edges of new possibilities. Failed projects, unresolved provocations, and refusals to produce are all signals that design, as pedagogy and praxis, is forever under negotiation. As Judith Butler observed in the aftermath of September 11, 2001, 14 Judith Butler, *Precarious Life: The Powers of Mourning and Violence* (Verso Books, 2004). critical voices challenging dominant narratives of war and security faced censorship, anti-

intellectualism, and the risk of being dismissed as hysterical. 15 In particular, Butler pointed to the dangerous re-emergence of rigid binaries—between "East" and "West," "civilization" and "barbarism"—that continue to shape political discourse today.

Butler's diagnosis of the silencing of dissent, and her warning against simplistic oppositions, resonate deeply in our current moment of linguistic exhaustion and political crisis. The difficulty of voicing critique—and the risks it carries—reflects one of the biggest challenges of design education in the present moment: how to create space for radical inquiry and intervention within institutions that often resist destabilization and dissent. If we take seriously the call to reimagine design education as a site of co-creative wor(l)d-making—that is, the generation of new vocabularies and their actualization—then it must also confront its own complicities and crises, committing to the invention of languages and practices capable of imagining otherwise.

To speak with a different voice, design education must become a space not only for producing "things" but for inventing new vocabularies *with* and *through* practice. This demands primarily a rethinking of the purpose of design schools, which cannot remain mere professional training grounds or capitalized knowledge-accumulation systems, focused on market-driven outputs or pre-defined skills. In the face of social collapse, ecological devastation, and epistemic exhaustion, design schools must become a site of ontological experimentation—a space where we question the very foundations of what is made, how, and why.

Part of what limits this potential is the persistent division between design education and design research. If research is treated as abstract, elite, and "publishable" while education is relegated to applied training, both become impoverished. If design is to contribute meaningfully to inventing other wor(l)ds, education must become inquiry, and research must be pedagogical. Classrooms, studios, and thesis labs should not be sites of transmission but of co-creation—spaces where students and educators collectively invent the languages and practices we need but do not yet have. This means, of course, involving students not as passive recipients of knowledge, but as active participants in wor(l)d-making.

16   About this topic, reference is always to: Paulo Freire, *Pedagogy of the Oppressed* (Herder and Herder, 1970). If, as Wittgenstein and Fry suggest, realities are shaped through language—the words we inherit, contest, and invent—then students must be empowered to interrogate, rewrite, and forge new vocabularies. Design education must cultivate the capacity to articulate what has no name yet, to challenge exhausted scripts like those of "sustainability," "innovation," or "progress," and to experiment with words that make other futures imaginable—and translatable into practice.

In a time of fragmentation and uncertainty, we are not just lacking in knowledge—we are lacking in ways to mobilize it, to put it into motion, to bring it to life in the world. As Donna Haraway beautifully wrote in her *Staying with the Trouble*: "It matters what we use to think other matters with; it matters what stories we tell to tell other stories with; it matters what knots knot knots, what thoughts think thoughts, what descriptions describe descriptions, what ties tie ties. It matters what stories make worlds, what worlds make stories." 17 Donna J. Haraway, *Staying with the Trouble: Making Kin in the Chthulucene* (Duke University Press, 2016), p. 12. Design, in this sense, is not just about shaping objects or systems—it's about shaping the narratives and imaginaries that allow those worlds to come into being. And to think in these terms— beyond isolated problems and into the collective mess of reality—requires a new "ecology of practice," 18 Isabelle Stengers, "Introductory Notes on an Ecology of Practices," *Cultural Studies Review* 11, no. 1 (2005): pp. 183–96, https://doi.org/10.5130/csr.v11i1.3459. as Isabelle Stengers reminds us. In this light, design education becomes not only a training ground for aesthetics or skills but a site of epistemological experimentation focussed on the relationship between the word and the world. What counts as knowledge? Who gets to produce it? How does form carry arguments? The classroom should not only transmit expertise but provoke doubt, expand vocabularies, and stretch the bounds of what thinking can look or feel like.

Adopting this approach means embracing uncertainty not as failure, but as material. It means legitimizing messiness, emotional labor, interdisciplinary collaboration, and favoring context over polish. The design school must become a site of social experimentation: not a talent pipeline, but a rehearsal space for different ways of knowing and making. Not to illustrate theory, but to incarnate it. To word what it's not yet sayable, and to design it for worlds yet to come.

Biasetton, Noemi. "In the 'Real World', Nothing Is Neutral: Design Schools, Conflict, and the Question of Palestine." *Villardjournal*. Quodlibet, 2025.

Buckley, Cheryl. "Made in Patriarchy: Toward a Feminist Analysis of Women and Design." *Design Issues* 3, no. 2 (1986): 3–14.

Butler, Judith. *Gender Trouble: Feminism and the Subversion of Identity*. Routledge, 2006.

Butler, Judith. *Precarious Life: The Powers of Mourning and Violence*. Verso Books, 2004.

Cross, Nigel. "Designerly Ways of Knowing." *Design Studies*, Special Issue Design Education, 3, no. 4 (October 1, 1982): 221–27.

Derrida, Jacques. *Of Grammatology*. Les Éditions de Minui, 1967.

Foucault, Michel. *L'archéologie Du Savoir*. Éditions Gallimard, 1969.

Freire, Paulo. *Pedagogy of the Oppressed*. Herder and Herder, 1970.

Fry, Tony. *Defuturing: A New Design Philosophy*. Bloomsbury Visual Arts, 2020.

Haraway, Donna J. *Staying with the Trouble: Making Kin in the Chthulucene*. Duke University Press, 2016.

Lee, Chris. *Immutable: Designing History*. Onomatopee, 2022.

Pater, Ruben. *The Politics of Design: A (Not So) Global Design Manual for Visual Communication*. BIS, 2016.

Stengers, Isabelle. "Introductory Notes on an Ecology of Practices." *Cultural Studies Review* 11, no. 1 (2005): 183–96.

Wittgenstein, Ludwig. *Philosophical Investigations*. Basil Blackwell, 1953.

Wittgenstein, Ludwig. *Tractatus Logico-Philosophicus*. Kegan Paul, Trench, Trubner & Co., 1922.

Set Margins' #79
WHEN WORDS FAIL
Knowledge Production Through
Practice-Based Art, Design, and Education

Editor
 Giulia Cordin

Contributing authors
 Nida Abdullah, Matteo Antoniazzi, Noemi Biasetton,
 Nitzan Cohen, Silvio Lorusso, Simone C Niquille,
 Kseniia (xè) Obukhova, Francesca Verga

Graphic design
 BIFFIPOL (with Chiara Branca)

Proofreader
 Ben Bazalgette

Printer
 Artigiana Grafica, Vicenza (Italy)

Image credits
 © unibz and the authors

Text rights
 © the authors

Rights over works
 © unibz

First edition, 2025
ISBN 978-90-835795-0-4

Set Margins'
www.setmargins.press

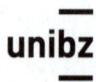